Shopping
The Insider's Way

Shopping
The Insider's Way

by Leil Lowndes

Citadel Press   Secaucus, New Jersey

Copyright © 1985 by Leil Lowndes

All rights reserved. No part of this book
may be reproduced in any form, except by
a newspaper or magazine reviewer who wishes
to quote brief passages in connection
with a review.

Published by Citadel Press
A division of Lyle Stuart Inc.
120 Enterprise Ave., Secaucus, N.J. 07094
In Canada: Musson Book Company
A division of General Publishing Co. Limited
Don Mills, Ontario

Queries regarding rights and permissions should be
addressed to Lyle Stuart, 120 Enterprise Avenue,
Secaucus, N.J. 07094

Manufactured in the United States of America

Library of Congress Cataloging in Publication Data

Lowndes, Leil.
   Shopping the insider's way.

   1. Shopping.   2. Consumer education.   I. Title.
TX335.L68   1985   640.73   85-17048
ISBN 0-8065-0939-2

Acknowledgments

This book is dedicated to the millions of ethical business and professional people in this country. It denounces the millions of less scrupulous ones. And it acknowledges with gratitude and respect the hundreds of the former who had the courage and candor to share with me the chicanery of the latter.

Finally, there are very special thanks to the many dozens of those who, over the years, have helped me to understand what it's like to be an "insider" and how to get a better deal from their industries.

And a warm thank you for a good friend whose ideas, time and support are reflected herein.

Contents

MOVING "Making Your Best Move"	13
BUYING A NEW CAR "Beating the Car Salesman at His Own Game"	22
BUYING JEWELRY "Getting a Gem Instead of Junk"	31
BUYING A HOUSE "Outbrokering Your Real Estate Broker"	38
BUYING CONTACT LENSES OR GLASSES "A Better View of Buying Glasses and Contact Lenses"	44
BUYING HOMEOWNER'S INSURANCE "Protecting Your Home (and Pocketbook) With Homeowner's Insurance"	48
GETTING BETTER AND LESS EXPENSIVE LEGAL SERVICES "Legal Services for Less, or Often You Are Your Own Best Lawyer"	53
HAVING YOUR HOUSE OR APARTMENT PAINTED "Getting the Best Paint Job—and the Best Price"	64
CAR REPAIR "Getting a Good Deal on Car Repair—Good Luck!"	69
GETTING STATIONERY OR A FLIER PRINTED "Cutting Your Printing Costs Up to 90 Percent"	75
CUTTING DOWN YOUR TELEPHONE BILL "Getting a Fair Shake from Ma Bell"	84

Contents

ADVERTISING YOUR PRODUCT ON THE RADIO "Getting Rock Bottom Prices for Radio Advertising"	94
TRAVEL SAVINGS "Saving Dollars on Travel"	100
BUYING A FUR "Getting a Great Fur for a Great Price"	112
PLANNING A FUNERAL "Cutting the High Cost of Dying (Funerals)"	121
CLEARING UP YOUR CREDIT RATING "Life in a Plastic Society, or How to Clear Up Your Credit Rating"	129
DINING OUT "Eating in Fine Restaurants—For Cheap"	134
RENTING A CAR "Hidden Treasure in the Trunk of Your Rental Car"	140
BUYING FOOD "Winning at the Food Game"	145
CHARTERING A BUS "Rent-A-Bus at the Pro's Price"	153
BUYING CAR INSURANCE "Insuring Rock Bottom Auto Insurance Rates"	158
CATERING A PARTY "How to Throw a Catered Party and Not Let It Throw You"	165
MAJOR PURCHASES—APPLIANCES, CAMERAS, STEREO, CLOTHING, ETC. "Major Savings on Major Purchases"	170
APPENDIX	181

Introduction

In your lifetime, you and your family in all probability will buy six cars, have four houses painted, make five moves, buy twelve insurance policies, four trips abroad and innumerable major appliances. In addition, you will dine at thousands of restaurants, engage half a dozen lawyers and buy food and telephone services every day.

THERE IS NO REASON YOU SHOULD PAY THE FULL PRICE FOR ANY OF THIS!

You are sitting with an insurance agent discussing your new policy. He's patiently explaining to you in layman's terms the advantages and disadvantages of certain riders to the policy he wants you to buy. The telephone rings. Your agent picks up the phone and his whole demeanor changes. He takes on a different attitude—he uses special words and speaks in an esoteric tongue—he begins to talk "insurance-ese" with the caller, a colleague in the insurance business.

Now you and I both know that if his comrade wanted to buy insurance from your agent, he'd get the finest policy for the very best price. The naïve would call it "professional courtesy." The enlightened realize it's really because they both "know the ropes" and one agent can't get away with pulling the wool over another agent's eyes.

In almost any industry, there are two prices on any goods or services—the insider's and yours. It makes perfect sense. If the vendor doesn't have to spend his time being super-salesman or psychologist—answering the endless stream of the novice's questions—he can afford to give his best price. When knowledgeable associates are buying his goods, he is happily reduced to nothing more than a purchasing agent. For very little work, he makes a small profit and is satisfied.

In buying, a little bit of knowledge can go a long way. If you have insight into your real estate broker's, your travel agent's and your jeweler's bottom line—if you are facile with some of the insider's words that your caterer and car salesman use—if you're savvy to the special techniques that your moving company and mechanic can use to bilk the unsuspecting—if you are on the lookout for your lawyer's methods for fattening his fee—*in short, if you know the ropes,* you will not get ripped off. The pro will assume that, since you have revealed your knowledge about some of the esoteric things in his industry, that you also know his best deal and rock bottom price. And that's exactly what you will get.

There are techniques to use, price codes in catalogues to crack, particular rip-offs to avoid, little-known extras to ask for and "buzz-words" to use that give you the knowledge and the cachet of the insider. All of these add up to a brand new way of buying which will get you a much better deal on any goods or services that you purchase.

Making Your Best Move

Packing up our lives and all our worldly goods and hauling that accumulation of years of living—whether it's across town or across the country—can be a pretty traumatic experience.

And, naturally, our free enterprise system has met the challenge with its usual mercenary flair. Gone are the days when you'd call a moving company and the owner/driver picked up the phone and said, "Yeah, when you movin' 'n' how much stuff ya got?" Now, a trained "Relocation Specialist" (usually a woman!) answers your call in soothing tones and gently guides you through the process of giving her far too much of your money. Moving has become big business, and extremely expensive, in our mobile society.

How do you beat the moving companies at their own game? Simply by knowing the ropes. Start where most good searches start—the Yellow Pages. Look at the ads. Some will be national companies, others are local. (If your move is local, you can probably save money by getting estimates from local trucking companies).

I'm going to tell you the next-cheapest way to move. (You know the first: Rent a U-Haul trailer or truck and "schlep-it-yourself.") If you're not up for that, however, pay close attention. Your first move is to call a good selection of moving companies and say, "Could you send me a brochure and a copy of your PERFORMANCE RECORD?" They may be taken aback because hardly anybody ever has the savvy to ask for it. However, the Interstate Commerce Commission requires that all van lines publish their "Report Card." It tells how many shipments the moving company made last year and how many complaints the ICC received about them. Get copies of these records from each company you are considering. If you prefer, you can get them directly from the ICC in Washington, D.C.

After the reviews are in, compare the companies' performance. Then call a few of the top-ranked movers and say, "I requested your performance record some weeks back and I think I'd like to get an estimate from your company." Right away they're going to be on their best behavior. I asked several movers how they would respond to this unusual type of approach and the response was a chorus of "I wouldn't screw around with that customer," "I'd pay special attention" and "I wouldn't want to mess that one up."

But here's the real clincher for saving yourself time and money: After you've gotten them on their toes by alluding to their performance record, and after you've told them when you're planning to move, where you're planning to move, and how many rooms of furniture you've got; then ask them, "Do you give BINDING ESTIMATES?" That's all you need to say. In fact, that's all you *should* say because you have just uttered the magic words— "binding estimate." This one question can make the difference between a three-thousand-dollar move and a five-thousand-dollar move because it prevents the movers from cheating. If they say, yes, they can give you a binding estimate, have the representative come to your home and appraise your situation.

Then you call the next van line and do the same thing. Repeat this procedure with three or four companies because estimates are free. The best deal to negotiate for is a "Not to Exceed" binding estimate. Ask for it up front too. This means that when your belongings are weighed, if they turn out to be heavier than estimated, you pay only the original quoted price. If they turn out to be lighter, the difference comes off your tab.

When the moving industry was deregulated in 1980, some companies, to get a competitive edge, started to give firm prices or "binding estimates." Others had to follow. But they all still hate like heck to do it. It's one of those deals where some companies won't bring it up, but if you request it, you'll probably get it. This type of estimate is crucial in calculating your true moving expenses. One "Relocation Specialist" I called said, yes, they gave binding estimates but had only granted one in the past year. "Why?" I asked. "Because nobody asked for it." Ask!

When the estimator comes to your door, tell him or her everything about your move, because even a binding estimate is not binding if there are any surprises after the move starts. When they find out your new apartment is on the top of a big hill in San Francisco and the truck can't make it up, and that it's a six-flight walk-up, they're going to be pretty mad and you can bet that will be reflected in the new charges in your bill. Tell them now because your estimated "accessorial" and "stair" charges are going to be less at this juncture when they're still competing for your business.

These are some of the possible extra charges that you should negotiate out now rather than paying through the nose for later:

ACCESSORIAL CHARGES—Will the truck be able to get right up to the door of "destination"? If not, you will pay for "shuttle service" or transferring your goods to a smaller vehicle that has access.

BRIDGE AND FERRY CHARGES—These are usual, but ask ahead of time what they will be.

STAIR, EXCESSIVE CARRY AND ELEVATOR CHARGES—That's self-explanatory. Movers consider time waiting for the elevator to be money.

WAITING TIME—Just make sure you are at "origin" and "destination" when the movers come so they don't have to wait. You don't want to pay $50/hour for them to entertain themselves listening to the truck radio. If you keep the boys waiting long enough at "destination," stuff goes into storage. And that's another study in rip-off.

BULKY ARTICLES—There are extra charges for transporting autos, boats, canoes and other such outsized items.

CARRYING CHARGES—Pianos, organs and other large possessions which require more care will be extra on your tab.

CRATING CHARGES—Do you have any valuable paintings or a grandfather clock that should be crated? Ditto for some major appliance. Either crate it yourself ahead of time or pay the pros top dollar.

EXTRA PICK UP OR DELIVERY—Are you picking up a sofa at Aunt Margie's house enroute to your new home, or are you planning on talking the driver into dropping the canoe off at your weekend place? Tell them now before their bloated "belated price" can take effect.

You might want to learn a little more "moverese" here so you can sound like you know the ropes. Like the bus companies, the moving van world talks in terms of ORIGIN and DESTINATION. It's simpler to say than "place I'm moving from" and "place I'm moving to."

An important question for you to consider is "How am I going to get my packing done?" The movers can do it (for a hefty fee) or you can do it. But if the packing is not done properly, the box could be rejected by the driver ("I ain't puttin' that flimsy thing on my truck") and it would have to be repacked (at a price arrived at after you're no longer in a strong bargaining position).

Best way to save money is for you to pack—properly. Do not use grocery and liquor store boxes. They fall apart. You can buy boxes and crates from the moving company. There's a markup but it might be worth it if they will buy them back later. You need only to ask. And if they won't, look in the Yellow Pages under "Boxes" and get your own.

Be aware that PBO boxes (those Packed By Owner) are a little more difficult to get insurance reimbursement for in case of damage. If there's a problem upon arrival, leave the box intact to show the damage from the outside. A good compromise might be for you to pack your non-fragile items and leave the china to the experts. Books are heavy. If you have a full library, it could pay to box them up and ship them to yourself at your new address at the post office's book rate.

If you do opt for the van boys to do some packing for you, keep an eye on them. Some of them enjoy playing BALLOON PACKING. That's packing the box half full, putting in a whole lot of padding, and charging you for a full box.

Once you've gotten your binding estimate, ask your estimator if she foresees any extra charges later. If she waffles on this point, pin her down to specific possibilities so all extra costs can be ruled out. Needless to say, don't cheat by hiding things from the estimator. You can't fool Mother Mover and, besides, she's taking full notes on everything.

You should know that if you're moving into another state, you must be prepared to spend more. If your move were one block shy of the state line, your tab would be appreciably less than to the same house on the other side of the state line. It has to do with the fact that interstate tariffs on file with the ICC are higher than the tariffs on file with the states. There's more competition from the small guys within the state.

Don't let the estimator just leave after giving you the moving price. Ask about insurance now. You might wind up with a low-ball move and a high-ball insurance policy. Get the numbers and factor them in. Ask about any perks the company offers. Some of the larger moving companies have become so marketing-conscious that they offer little frills like arranging a Welcome Wagon to greet you in your new neighborhood, and some big bonuses like discount airline tickets.

Once you've compared performance records, prices and perks of the different companies, you make your choice and you are given an "Order for Service." Read the fine print and reconfirm all charges. You will then be given what they call a DELIVERY SPREAD. That's the time between the date they are picking up your stuff to the time it's going to be delivered. Make a note that if they do not deliver "within the spread," ICC rules state that you can put your motel tab and half your food costs on their account. Delays are common, but a lot of people who don't know the rules sleep huddled in their coats on the floor of their empty new house when they could be enjoying the sauna at their local Ramada Inn.

When the "boys" come to make the move, be prepared for a chaotic scene. One hulk will be passing judgment on your furniture and shouting out at another who will be making hieroglyphic notations on the inventory sheet. Here's the cracked code.

BE	bent
BR	broken
BU	burned
CH	chipped
CU	contents and condition unknown
D	dented
G	gouged
MI	mildewed
MO	motheaten
SC	scratched

T   torn
W   worn
Z   cracked

Before you sign that, look it over carefully. What may be G to them may be only SC by you, and if it gets gouged during the move, you will lose any claim.

If you're only moving from one side of town to the other, you'll probably be charged by the number of hours the move takes. You can usually negotiate a maximum time charge. Your success depends on several factors—how competitive the market, your negotiating skill and the time of year. If it's all the same to you, move in the winter. You'll get a better deal from both local and long distance movers because there is less demand then.

Long distance movers either tally their tab by volume and density, or by weight (most prevalent). Unless they are bound by their estimate, there will be a gaping blank space in your BILL OF LADING (your receipt and details of the contract). The blank to be filled in is the LONG HAUL CHARGE—the cost based on the weight of the load.

That's a pretty big blank—one that leaves a lot of room for accidental and deliberate cheating. That's why you should have gotten a binding estimate, preferably a "Not to Exceed" estimate. However, there is a way to prevent cheating. Your cost is calculated by first weighing the empty truck (that's the TARE WEIGHT) and then reweighing it filled with your possessions. You can ask your mover when and where the "tare weight is going to be determined." Drive out to the scales at that time and watch them do the weighing. Are the tanks full of gas? If not, they could be filled before the next weigh-in and logged as a thousand pounds of "your possessions" that you're paying to move. How many men are in the van at weighing time? Will they be the same ones at the next weigh in? (You don't want to pay for the new driver's beer belly.) What about all those heavy dollies and other loading equipment? They should be on-board at the first weighing.

Then follow the truck to your house, monitor the loading and follow the truck back to the weigh station to make sure that your chattels are the only difference between tare weight and final weigh-in. The very fact that you are there will probably daunt any dishonest movers.

Now, when you get to your new house, the temptation is to be inside your new home excitedly directing the placement of all the furniture. Resist! This could be the most critical moment of the move. As each thing comes off the truck, one of the van men checks the condition as it goes into the house. You should be right by his side ticking things off on your inventory sheet, checking for damage, and making sure his inventory matches yours. Note any damage that he doesn't agree with on his inventory sheet before you sign it. Even then, it's a good idea to scribble something like "subject to unpacking" or "future inspection" on the document. A claim later for damaged or missing goods is much more difficult if the mover's inventory sheet doesn't have a notation. You have nine months to file a claim, but the sooner you file, the better chance you have of recovering any loss.

Take a peek inside the truck as the last item comes off to make sure the truck's empty.

Then, you'll prove yourself to be wise beyond your experience if you have arranged to pay by credit card. This is a smart move because if you find any unpleasant surprises in your unpacking, payment can be held up until the wrong is righted. Moving companies are pretty cagey, however, and you'll find most of them insisting on cash, money order or certified check. That's why it's so important to clear the stars out of your eyes and make clear judgments on the condition of your worldly goods as they come off the truck.

Tipping? Optional, but if you have had the poor chaps move your china cabinet and dining room table around three times trying to decide which way it looks best, they deserve a little bounty. And if all has gone well with your move, it will be a near miracle and you'll want to reward *somebody*.

Beating the Car Salesman at His Own Game

Most people break out in a cold sweat each time they realize it's time to turn in their old heap and buy a new car. They picture the by-now-familiar scene of themselves sitting across the desk, eager and emotional, desperately hoping they are getting a good price from the crafty salesman who is throwing figures at them. But, alas, most people know in their hearts that, no matter how smart they may be, when haggling with a car salesman they are but little guppies pitted against a shark. "After all," they complain to themselves, "he deals with the likes of me every day—several times each day. And I only purchase a car once every four or five years." Yes, you are right. One has reason to be nervous about the negotiation, because many car salesmen deserve their reputation of using every trick in the book to separate man or woman from his money.

This chapter is going to show you how to stand your ground and get the best possible price on any car you decide to purchase. You are going to learn how to reduce that slick scalper to nothing more than a *purchasing agent*—which is all he should be. And purchasing agents are not paid the whopping commissions that car salesmen try to extract from you. Let's plan your counter-attack one step at a time.

SQUARE ONE—PSYCHOLOGICAL PREP: Like an actor who does a few minutes of "prep" before walking out on a

Broadway stage, let's get you into the right frame of mind for this big purchase. Car manufacturers spend millions of dollars in advertising each year to get us to fall in love with an image. Cars are named after beautiful birds and other exotic animals—Firebird, Skylark, Cougar, Bobcat, Impala, Pinto, Mustang.... We fantasize ourselves in the TV commercial, either curvacious or virile, with the Colorado sunset gleaming through our hair, miraculously overcoming all odds as we drive our Detroit-made chariot straight up a mountainside. Every man who has ever been to an Auto Show subconsciously assumes that the car comes with the dazzling half-clad beauty draped across the hood—and no extra cost for that "option."

Cut! You are not buying a new image or lifestyle. You are buying *transportation*—and the choice of car should be as devoid of emotions as you can possibly manage. Your first step is to perform a voluntary lobotomy and cut away all such susceptibility to image. Every car differs greatly in acceleration, ride, parking ease, safety features, comfort, cargo space, servicing—and the list goes on and on.

SQUARE TWO—DECIDE EXACTLY WHICH CAR YOU WANT: It is time to sit down and have a long conversation with yourself and your family to decide what features are important to you. Analyze your needs so you can customize the ideal car for you. Are you short or tall?—it affects your visibility needs. Do you travel a lot with luggage?—if you do you should avoid thief-tempting hatchback cars. How important is mileage to you?—both *Consumer Reports* and the EPA publish average mileages on all current cars.

Compare prices, but don't panic when you see the published price. In a few more minutes of reading, you will know that the list price is *not* what you are going to pay. You're going to learn how to get rid of the markup which ranges from about 10 percent on economy cars up to 25 percent on luxury cars.

Give yourself enough lead time. Do not wait until your old car is towed to the graveyard before you decide to buy. If you're under the gun to buy immediately, the salesman will smile and say, "Have I got a deal for you!" He sure does, and you're going to pay dearly for your rush. If you have the luxury of choosing when to buy, you can negotiate a better price. Try the middle of the winter. It's slim pickings for the dealers and they are more anxious to make a sale. You might also score a little higher at the end of each month, when quotas are tallied.

Probably the best place to start is with *Consumer Reports*. You can narrow your choice from the vast array of temptations down to two or three cars before you ever enter a showroom. The first consideration you might make is which size car you want—small, compact, medium, large, sporty or a small van.

This is just the first of many decisions you will make. Consumers Union (the publisher of *Consumer Reports*) actually purchases about 35 cars a year incognito and then puts them through grueling tests. The cars are judged in every conceivable way—road tests, track tests, shop analysis. They even test comfort by packing as many engineers as will fit into the car and then asking them how they feel.

The results of hundreds of tests and comparisons are published in the April issue of *Consumer Reports* each year. If there's even a chance of a new car being in your budget next year, make a note on your April calendar to pick up a copy. (People have a nasty habit of stealing that issue from libraries.)

One other helpful publication in choosing a car is *The Wall Street Journal*. Every Friday each model's production figures are published. Zero production can mean oversupply, therefore lower prices.

SQUARE THREE—INITIAL VISIT TO DEALER: After you've narrowed your choice to several cars, the time has come to visit a dealer—*not to buy*, but to check out your research and see if you are comfortable with your initial choices. Before this trip, call a few of the larger dealers and see if they have the models you are considering on the lot. When you enter the showroom for this first time, announce that you are here this time to look, not to buy. Don't let the salesman pressure you into any discussion of purchase. (After all, you haven't decided that this is the dealer you want to buy from yet.) If it is a good dealership, the salesman will let you spend a little time with each car and even take a test drive. (It's a good idea to visit in the early morning or early afternoon on a rainy day to ensure that they will have more time for your browsing.) You can ask the dealer for a copy of the sticker price to take with you. That's the piece of paper taped to the window with all the inflated numbers on it. If, after the test drive, you are able to narrow down your choice to one or two cars, it's time to go to Square Four.

SQUARE FOUR—LEARN THE DEALER'S BOTTOM LINE: Now is the time to do a little correspondence course homework which will enable you to beat the salesman at his own game. The biggest bargaining advantage he has is that he knows his bottom line and you don't. Thanks to Consumers Union, and companies like Car/Puter (1603 Bushwick Avenue, Brooklyn, N.Y. 11207), you have the ability to learn that all-important bottom line too. These are a couple of the organizations which, for a small fee, will give you the actual price the dealer paid the manufacturer for the car—in other words, his bottom line. Consumers Union (Dept. DCB-LF, 256 Washington Street, Mt. Vernon, N.Y. 10553), arms you with what is called in the business INVOICE PRICE—that is, the to-the-penny price that your dealer paid the manufacturer for the car. The printout also comes with the invoice price of the rainbow of options available—power windows, tinted glass, courtesy lights, air-conditioning.... Practically anything manufacturers can think of to raise the tab is an option. Read the advantages, disadvantages and Consumers Union's comments and recommendations on each in *Consumer Reports*. They'll tell you just how important their engineers feel it is to have a remote control outside mirror or a little heater in the seat to warm your bottom in the winter. Look at the costs and decide what you desperately need, what you want, and what you can live happily ever after without. Then, like a kid putting together a house with tinker toys, "customize" your car.

Now the arithmetic. Add the "base price" of the car to the options—all at cost, remember. And then add the "destination charge" on the sticker. That's the dealer's cost for having the car shipped to him. (You'll also receive it in your printout.) You now have the all-important negotiating tool, the Invoice Price.

Unlike a poker game where if you get out, you lose, there is a winning way out of the car-buying game. If you don't have the stomach for negotiating, there are several services which guarantee that, if you know exactly the car you want, they will put you in touch with a dealer who will give it to you for $125 above the dealer's cost. You must know *exactly* what you want, however, so you don't hassle them with questions; time is money, remember. Those of you who choose this course, do not go to Square Five. Repair instead to a car buying service like Car/Puter. Check your local Yellow Pages or Chamber of Commerce. Beware, however, that the participating dealer may not be the closest one to your home and thereby cause problems with servicing later.

Courageous negotiators who want a foolproof scheme, read on.

SQUARE FIVE—CHOOSE YOUR DEALER: You are now ready to choose the lucky man who will make only a few hundred dollars from you. But don't feel bad. If all goes according to plan, he'll put in under an hour's work.

Auto-owning friends' and relatives' recommendations are the first source in your search. When you get a name, further check out the dealer's reputation: call the Better Business Bureau and see if any complaints have been lodged. Another consideration is that you want a dealer nearby so that you don't have huge towing charges in case there is a problem.

Look for a dealer with a service area two to three times as large as his showroom. Ask if he has diagnostic equipment such as an oscilloscope (a computer engine analyzer that can save hefty labor costs in analyzing your car's problem). Don't be hesitant to ask for the names of some satisfied customers and do a little personal research.

SQUARE SIX—THE NEGOTIATION: Here's the fun part. You enter the showroom armed with the heavy artillery; in your hip pocket you have the printout of his invoice price. As the editorial director of *Consumer Reports* told me, your mantra should be "Deal from the Invoice Up." Most salesmen will start with the sticker price. You will negotiate. He will out-negotiate you. People who do not know the invoice price are manipulated through many clever, worn-out but still effective sales techniques. They walk out fantasizing that they might have a good deal because they were able to talk him down a few hundred dollars from the list price. Pyrrhic victory.

All this unpleasant haggling can be obviated by one succinct speech delivered by you. You look 'em straight in the eyes and say, "*Look, I'm shopping for cost. I have visited (or will visit unless you can give me a good price) other showrooms. I've customized exactly the car I want and I'm willing to wait for it. How much over invoice do you require for this car?*" You hand him the list with the same confidence that you would lay four aces out on the card table.

Further, you tell the dealer that you want the total price inclusive of any fees or taxes. "*After we've made a deal, I don't want any extra charges thrown in.*" Let him know, in a polite way, that you are looking for the best deal—that you definitely intend to buy but, if he can't meet your price, you will go somewhere else.

If at this point he tries to bring trading in your old car into the negotiation, tell him that you look at that as a separate transaction and, "*Let's take care of this one first.*"

The markup you are seeking—this is profit plus overhead—

should be in the $150-$400 range. Anything over that, and you move on to the next dealer. About $200 over *invoice* is a good deal for both of you. Shoot for it.

I should mention here that, because of limited supply, these markups do not apply to Japanese cars and certain other imports. It's a seller's market on Toyotas, Hondas, Nissans, and Mazdas.

Back to American cars. Any wise dealer will recognize that he can make a decent profit with this markup and all he has to do is order your car from the factory exactly to your specifications. Most purchasing agents would be thrilled to earn $200 in one hour.

SQUARE SIX AND ONE-HALF—TRICKS TO BEWARE OF! Even if they agree to the low markup, some dealers have some tricks up their sleeves to get more money out of you. Here are a few of the more famous ones to be wary of. Forewarned is forearmed!

The old "Low Ball": The dealer agrees to your price but says, "Since it is such an unprecedented low price, I'll have to get approval from my superior." He then leaves you to sweat alone for awhile. Five minutes later he returns saying that his manager couldn't approve such a small tab. Or he'll tell you that you have to talk with his boss. His "boss" is a professional "closer" who will use any number of maneuvers to get you to agree to the increased price—including making you feel sorry for the "nice salesman" who mistakenly consented to the low price.

The way to avoid this one is to see it coming. Tell your salesman before he leaves the room "for consultation" that it's a no-go if there's any change in price.

Another famous "Low Ball" they sling is this. He adds up his figures incorrectly to come in with a low price and get you to agree. Then he checks his figures. Whoops! He then comes up with a higher "correct" price. Suckers usually fall for this one because they've already bought the car psychologically.

Or he'll actually go to contract at the low price and then, about the time your car should be in and you're all hot and lathered up for it, he'll call and tell you it will be a few months longer. But he just "happens to have" a similar one on the lot that costs a few hundred more. What do you want to bet it's your car that he's added a few options to? Tell him no, and you'll be amazed how soon your corrected car comes in.

Another scam to watch out for is a variation of the above. You've waited a long time for your car. It finally comes in, but he tells you, "It came in with some extra options by mistake. You can either buy those or wait a few more months for your car."

Or, how's this one? "The truck your car was on had an accident. But we just happen to have...?

The best defense against this type of dirty pool is to not wait until your old car is ready for the junkyard before buying a new one. Let the dealer know you've got some time and he'll be less apt to pull these nasty rabbits out of his hat.

There's more: Be on guard if, in the midst of your negotiations, the dealer offers you a "private room where you and the Mrs. can talk it over." Illegal though it may be, these rooms have been known to be bugged.

Another favorite ruse is to add a hundred or so dollars on the price as routinely as sales tax. The charge is called "Dealer Preparation." This "prep" charge is the dealer's fee for giving the car a once-over before delivering it to you. With few exceptions, this price is built into the cost. Some manufacturers such as Ford, Chrysler and GM even reimburse the dealer. If he tries to hit you with a prep charge, give him an emphatic, "No, that was not discussed in our original agreement." Make a fuss and they'll take it off.

They may try to charge for "undercoating" or "rustproofing" as though it's de rigueur. It's definitely not. It's an option and not a highly recommended one at that. "Advertising" cost is another deceptive charge which you should see through. If they try this one, remind them that you accepted the car on the basis of a firm price.

And be sure to ask ahead of time for a confirmation that the price you were quoted is the absolutely final tab. A few small charges such as initial gas and oil charge, or title and inspection fees are legitimate, but make sure they're spelled out up front.

SQUARE SEVEN—THE CONTRACT: When, and *only* when, all wrinkles are ironed out and you've both agreed upon a final price, you sign the contract. Don't let your dealer rush you. Read it slowly and carefully, making sure there are no empty spaces which could be filled in later. The contract should permit you to cancel the deal if any extra costs are added. If that statement's not there, write it in for you both to sign!

SQUARE EIGHT—GETTING THE CAR: Your new car has just arrived and now is the time to invest a final but very important two hours in your car. Before you take delivery, take it on a test drive and have your salesman ride with you. If he balks, take the manager. Some authorized person from the dealership should be with you so he can give you a written confirmation of any defects. Look over the body and the insides in bright daylight—give it a complete inspection. Check for defects in the paint, squeaky brakes, rattles, etc. Make sure everything works right—even test the air-conditioner although it may be below zero outside. Your bargaining power takes a big dip once you've accepted the car. You go from being a valued new customer to an old griping one who demands warranty work which brings your dealer no profit. Get everything fixed now while the dealer is anxious to get your car off his lot.

So, little guppies in the car buying game can grow into big fish when they feed upon knowledge. It is my fervent wish that this chapter will enable you to bare your jaws at the shrewdest of the car-selling sharks.

Getting a Gem Instead of Junk

Ever hear of honor among thieves? Pay attention: I am not saying that people in the jewelry business are thieves. I am saying that there are higher markups and there is more room for confusion in buying gems and fine jewelry than in almost any other large-scale consumer business. There is very little protection for the buyer. The smart ones get gems, the stupid get junk. Or they pay at least twice as much for the good stuff.

Before I tell you how to appear knowledgeable and experienced in buying jewelry, and how to haggle successfully (even with your local jeweler), let me tell you a little about the epicenter of the jewelry universe—New York's diamond district. In a single square block bordered by Fifth and Sixth Avenues, 47th and 48th Street, a good percentage of the world's jewelry dealing takes place. Through one building alone, 580 Fifth Avenue, three-quarters of the world's diamonds pass at one time or another. There are insurance policies that are valid for that one block only. One dealer told me that he tried to take an associate to a popular restaurant nearby. They got to the corner and his friend came to a screeching halt. He couldn't cross the street carrying his gems because he would not be insured one step out of the diamond district.

If, with the enormous amounts of treasures and gelt (Yiddish for "money" —Yiddish is a close second to English in the district) changing hands, the district had to depend on the usual laws and law enforcement system in this country, there would be no diamond district. Instead there would be erected a gigantic block-square jailhouse. But, because of the unique system of honor that has developed, the jewelry dealers have become some of the most uncorrupt, trustworthy and reliable vendors in the world—to each other.

Literally hundreds of thousands of dollars in gems are loaned around the market on a handshake. Some dealers keep a memorandum book, but that's just for, as it says, remembering. Remembering who they gave that little 225-thousand-dollar bauble to.

How did this phenomenally principled society develop? Easy. There is no place for such liberal expressions as "give him a second chance," "the guy meant well," "it won't happen again." In this league, you break your word and they break your legs and you never deal again. So, by process of elimination, you have some guys who are pretty straight-shooters when dealing with each other.

Dealing with *you*, it's a different story. If you look like you have a little wool shade on your forehead, they'll be only too happy to pull it down right over your eyes. So let's brush up on how to look 'em right in the whites of their eyes and deal like they do. If you can get to New York and feel comfortable holding your own with a diamond dealer on the block, there are some pretty substantial savings to be had. A wholesaler's or diamond district's mark-up to insiders is more in the 25 percent range than 300 percent. My advice, if you get to the Big Apple, is to start at the big prestigious stores where their personnel are trained to take time with shoppers. Get a clear idea from them what you are looking for. Then visit *the block*. What you do there, is go from dealer to dealer and see whom you can get the best price from.

The following counsel also goes for dealing with jewelers anywhere in the country. Except for strictly retail jewelry shops, the price you pay can be inversely proportional to how much the jeweler thinks you know. There's even a way to get a better price from your neighborhood jeweler. Read on.

If you're considering a serious gem purchase, first thing to do is invest in a LOUPE. A loupe is a small, round magnifying glass that jewelers put in their eye to spot imperfections or INCLUSIONS as they are called in the business. You can pick a loupe up for about $25 at a jewelry-supplies store or mail-order business. "Ten-X" is the standard for the industry. Practice with the loupe at home before you take it to the store. Put it to your eye and move the gem, not the loupe or both as the uninitiated do. The trick is to keep the loupe stuck to the eye and move the gem until it comes into focus.

Let's say you are shopping for a diamond ring. Let your fingers do the walking through the Yellow Pages for jewelers—wholesale. If you look knowledgeable, it's not in their best interest to check your credentials as you walk through the door. They want to sell as much as you want to buy. If there is no wholesale dealer in your town, you can use the same technique on a jewelry shop. The most important thing to remember is do *not* buy the ring already made. Buy the diamond separately and have it mounted. There are several reasons for this. One, you don't know how much the stone weighs (how many carats it is) when it's mounted. Two, you can't see the inclusions or color as well in the mounting. And three, sometimes a jeweler will place the prongs in a position to cover up some inclusions (also called GLETZ).

Talk in terms of carats. Once you learn how the insiders describe quality, your opening salvo to the jeweler will be to ask how much he charges for a certain quality of diamond, per carat. Then you ask him to show you some STONES. Important: Say "Stones," not diamonds. If the jeweler is good, he'll show you at least three of relatively equal weight. If he doesn't, ask for more so you'll have a basis of comparison. Ask for a piece of white paper and his tweezers. Fold the white paper in two, then open it half way. One by one, place the stones *upside down* on the paper. When you're discussing the parts of the diamond with the jeweler, the top is called the TABLE, next to it is the CROWN, the widest part is the GIRDLE. Then comes the slant, the PAVILION, to the bottom tip called the CULET. You pick up the stone with his tweezers and move it to your eye.

There are three "c's" you are looking for: color, clarity and cut. First, color. This is best judged on the white paper. The ideal is colorless ranging down to the least desirable yellow. If it shows color, say the stone looks a bit CAPE. Cape is a word taken from the Cape of South Africa, where a lot of yellow diamonds were mined. If you're not happy with what he's showing you, ask "What have you got that's FINER?" The word here is "finer," not "better" or "nicer." Don't ask me why. That's just the way they talk. Look through the back, the "pavilion," for color. Look through the pavilion and the "table" for flaws.

There are two simple scales for you to familiarize yourself with so you can converse with the jeweler more accurately. Naturally, the more yellow (or "cape"), and flawed the stone is, the cheaper. The parentheses on the clarity scale enclose the lingo used by the insiders. Don't worry about it, however. You're not trying to tell the jeweler that you're in the business. Just that you know what you're talking about.

COLOR SCALE

Colorless
Near Colorless
Slightly Tinted
Very Light Yellow
Light Yellow
Fancy Yellow

CLARITY SCALE

Internally Flawless (If)
Very Very Slightly Included (VVS)
Very Slightly Included (VSI)
Slightly Included (SI)
Imperfect (I)

The shapes of the stones are fairly self-explanatory: ROUND, OVAL, PEAR, EMERALD (a rectangle with little cut-off edges) and MARQUISE (oval with two points).

Here are a few more widely used terms before we go on to other jewelry. There are several euphemisms for the flaws in a stone. GLETZ is one big flaw. FEATHERS is a lot of little ones. If you see a NEST, you're seeing a grouping of small inclusions. Doesn't a SILVER CAPE diamond sound nice? When your jeweler is selling you the yellowish stone, he'll call it that. If he were buying it, he'd say, "No, it's too CAPE. I want less color."

Flaws are flaws but color is a matter of opinion. Even the experts don't always agree on exact color category. If you're buying opals, rubies, emeralds, jade, sapphires, even diamonds, take someone with a good sense of color. Color perception varies greatly. Sad but true, a lot of old diamond-district lifers have to put themselves out to pasture because color sense can diminish with age. Some medication also affects color judgment. If you're not sure of yours, take an artistic friend or cousin shopping with you. Artists and designers usually have a keen sense of color. Advanced technology has entered the world of jewelry. Many jewels, including almost all pink pearls, are color treated. The treatment is detectable only by laboratory equipment.

Color may be debatable but size is not. It's not advisable too early in your negotiations, but, after you've looked at several stones and inquired about carat size, ask your jeweler if he can bring out his scale (carat-weighing scale) so you can start weighing them. Then put each stone in the little dish and you'll know the exact carat size.

If you're buying other types of jewelry, such as bracelets, earrings or chains, your neighborhood jeweler can be your best bet. Don't buy from his stock of jewelry, however. Here's the gambit. Ask to see his complete selection of whatever treasure you want. Then, ask for his catalogues. It's not feasible for your jeweler to keep an extremely large stock. There's no interest being earned on these expensive trinkets in his safe. So the jewelers do a lot of ordering from the manufacturers. Try to spend some time with his catalogues.

Each bauble has a number and a price. The usual price in the catalogue can be three times what your jeweler pays. That's right—*three* times his cost. You can check that by looking in the front of the catalogue. It may say the price is TRIPLE KEYSTONE. Some catalogues say the price is KEYSTONE. That still means double.

My diamond district guru told me that he took a friend of his around the market to help him buy a ring. When they found what they liked, the maven (Yiddish for expert) said, "Give me the K on that." The seller told him the price, and the purchase was made. When the two got up to my mentor's office, he handed over the ring and asked for precisely half of the quoted price. "Why just half?" asked his friend. Because "the K" is the codeword in the district for Keystone—or twice the price.

Knowing your jeweler's price puts you in a tremendous bargaining position. Pointing to a $900 treasure in his catalogue, you can say to him, "Look, you'll be paying about $300 for that. I'll give you $500. That's $200 for you." Very few good businessmen will turn down $200 for just placing an order. And you'll be saving up to $400 depending on the "discount" he might have offered you. If you see something you like, you can ask to see similar things in his manufacturer's catalogue. That exercise will let you know about what he paid for the item you like.

Another game plan for the relatively ruthless is this: Note the page number of your chosen trinket. Then turn to the front of the book. It will tell you by page who the manufacturer is. You can call the manufacturer direct. He'll try to talk you into ordering more than one item, but you usually will get your order filled.

Getting a Gem Instead of Junk

Perhaps you are interested in a piece of old jewelry (called an ESTATE PIECE) that is not in any catalogue. If you are unsure of the price, you can purchase it and take it to an appraiser. Any reputable jeweler should permit this and accept its return if it is valued at far less than he has advertised it to be. However, make sure it is an independent appraiser you are taking it to, not one recommended by the jeweler you brought it from. And even then, take the appraisal with a grain of salt. As my diamond district confidante said, "Nobody can know the current price of everything. It changes every day. Unless you're out there on the street dealing daily, there's no way you could know. An appraiser is a salaried laborer sitting behind his loupe. What does he really know?"

What about gems as investments? Not so hot, I've been told. But for keeping— "A thing of beauty is a joy forever." And it is a bigger joy if you've been able to talk your way into getting a big bargain.

Outbrokering
Your Real Estate Broker

The single largest purchase most of us make is our home. And the sad fact is that most people grasp the broker's hand and submissively trail him through the perilous home-buying labyrinth. Like lambs to a slaughter we bleat our few questions and trust that the broker is working for us.

Poppycock! Make no mistake. The broker is working for the seller. Actually, he's working for number one—himself; number two—the seller; and we, the buyers, come in a poor third. This is backwards, because we buyers control the purse-strings by our ability to say "yes" or "no." Therefore, we should hold the best cards.

This chapter will show you how to do just that, and turn the tables when you're buying a house. I'm not going to attempt to demystify the subtleties of equity financing or easements and restrictive covenants. You should have your banker, broker and lawyer do that. But I *am* going to give you a few tactics and hints for getting a better deal on your house.

Your first step, after deciding where you want to live and how much you can afford (the experts say a house costing two and one-half times your annual salary is your ceiling) is to find a few good brokers. That's right, a few good brokers. This is done by asking any friends you have in the area—or talk to people puttering in their garden, the local librarian, grocery store managers, gas pumpers, sales clerks and bartenders. A community grapevine is pretty sinewy stuff and most people in a burg will have heard who is reputable and who is not.

A real estate agent works solely on commission from the sale. He or she receives a percentage of whatever money can be extracted from you to pay for the house. This means that the broker has no vested interest in getting the house for you at a lower price, other than not wanting to lose you as a customer.

But I am going to introduce you to a sure-fire way to get a broker to be really interested in getting a good deal for you. It has to do with the multiple listing system. Your broker probably has three kinds of listings. They are called EXCLUSIVE, LISTING AGENCY and MULTIPLE listings.

EXCLUSIVE, of course, means that only your broker has that listing. Exclusive listings are hard to get. After all, why shouldn't a seller put as many people as possible to work for him since the seller's fee is not affected by which broker finds the buyer?

LISTING AGENCY is what we'll call a "primary" listing. It means that this particular agency got the first listing and then shared it with other brokers by putting it on the multiple listings list. In other words, the seller came to your man and he's the broker who gets to plop his sign in front of the house. If your agent sells you either one of his exclusive or listing agency houses, he hits the jackpot because he gets the whole commission.

MULTIPLE LISTING means somebody else got the listing first but your broker can show it to you. If he sells you this house, he has to split the commission with the accomplice who got the primary listing.

You're probably getting the point by now. In case you haven't, here it is: Your broker is going to be a heck of a lot more interested in selling you his "exclusive" or "listing agency" homes than those from his "multiple listings" list because he gets the whole pie. The tactic is to tell the broker the following. *"I want you to show me your exclusive or listing agency homes only. Don't waste your time showing me your multiple listings."*

He may be a little confused by this unique approach, but tell him not to worry about it, you know what you're doing. And you do! Because your broker is making double the commission he would get on an ordinary multiple listing, he's going to be in a position to pass on some good savings to you.

For instance: You've found a house, you love it a lot, but you and the seller are still two thousand dollars apart on price. You can tell your broker, "Absorb the difference from your commissions and it's a sale." This would be impossible if the broker's only getting 3½ percent from a house he sold as a multiple listing. But if he's getting a full 7 percent on a hundred-thousand-dollar house, that gives him seven thousand dollars to play with. He desperately wants you to buy before some other broker who found the house on the multiple listing jumps the gun and finds a fanatic who will pay the full asking price—thereby cutting his percentage in half.

When you use this unusual and effective tactic, however, you must appear to practically close your eyes and cover your ears as the broker drives you past houses he has listed only as multiples. (If the house interests you, sneak a peek at the name of the listing agency on the sign, however, because that will be your next call.) The reason for not asking him about any house which he only has as a "multiple" is because in the extremely competitive real estate business, "Who Showed You the House First" is a very, very big deal. And any agent who tries to sell you a house that was shown to you previously by another agent is going to get a severe form of whatever punishment is prevalent in his hamlet, whether it's having his kneecaps busted or his name blackened forever.

You then go to the next agent and repeat the performance. You may think this is more troublesome than it's worth. Well, it's worth a lot because if your broker has a special interest in selling to you, there are numerous ways he can make you happy and save you money during the inevitable sensitive negotiations to follow. Since your man is the broker who has the seller's ear, he can convince him that you're the winner. He can hold other buyers at bay even though you've made a lower offer. He can help you with financing, repairs, absorb some closing costs and make housebuying a whole lot happier for you in a myriad of ways. Now you've got him working for you!

If you don't follow this advice and go with an affable broker that you like or otherwise feel is your guy, great. But you might be paying for the friendship. Your defense could be, "Well, he's got all the houses on multiple listing and he wants the sale, so he's working for me." That's approaching accuracy, but here's the rub. Unless a house is his exclusive or primary listing, he doesn't have contact with the owner. The chap who got the first listing (and vastly prefers to sell the house himself) does. Also, since your favorite broker will only be getting half the commission, he has very little room to give you any bargains.

Sad but true, you probably should not take your broker into total confidence, since he wants you to pay as much as possible to up his commission. If your real bottom line on a price is that you will not go over $80,000, you should probably hint that around $75,000 is tops for you. That way when he confides that to his client, as of course he will, you still have a little leeway. Just remember, very few houses ever go for the asking price. Like a Hollywood luminary's age and weight, the price of a house is a very subjective matter. It is to a great extent determined by negotiation.

I have found that there is little difference between independent brokers and the national franchises. The franchises will say, "nay," there is a lot of important training and information that the biggies provide. I asked about training courses, etc., and found that some of their best courses are marvelous ones in motivation and how to be a better salesman. Great!

However, franchise folk seemed genuinely pleased with the services offered. One ex-broker I spoke with told me that when a big national real estate chain came into town, he was approached with the age-old, "Join me or I'll putcha outta business." Well, he's outta business now. Makes sense. The giants have a lot of clout, computerized listings, and some even are getting into videotapes of houses so you can "see" them without leaving the broker's office.

Your broker may be the star of the house-purchasing show, but there can be a big supporting cast of bankers, lawyers, engineers, inspectors, appraisers, surveyors, insurance agents and even termite tracers. You can ask your broker for recommendations on the above, but keep in mind that kickbacks are not unheard of in this industry, so get a "second opinion." Also, you should do some pretty fancy finger and phone work from the Yellow Pages, interviewing potential bankers, lawyers, engineers, inspectors, appraisers, surveyors, insurance agents and termite tracers.

There are very few shortcuts in housebuying. Choosing good professionals to help you is the second most important thing to choosing the right house. Handpick a good back-up team. And when you make your final offer, be sure to have "subject to inspection" put on it. That way you are protected if your pros (such as your engineer who's inspecting the structure) come up with any nasty surprises. And do your own detective work.

Here's a bit of trivia. When you're choosing your castle, in addition to checking the roof, the plumbing, the heating system, the basement, etc., you should check out the underside of the toilet tank cover. You read right. It's a good way to see if you're getting the straight story on how old the house is. There's a 90 percent chance you will see the date the plumbing was put in etched there for posterity.

Outbrokering Your Real Estate Broker

One of the naughtiest things a broker can do is not disclose problems to you. Open up lines of communication with the owner. Ask him why he's moving and hope he comes up with a good answer. Ask for copies of the past utility bills and tax records. If there hasn't been a recent tax increase, you can be pretty sure you'll get one. When you decide to buy, make the seller your friend, not adversary. Get any service contracts or manuals he has on appliances. Get the house plans if they still exist, and recommendations on local carpenters, plumbers and all those folk you're sure to have to deal with at some time or another.

I would be remiss if I said that, after reading this chapter, you are ready to embark on the perilous house-buying journey. Invest some time in deep research on mortgages, insurances, inspections, warranties, settlement costs, etc. If I started with the details here, your feet would go to sleep in about 10 minutes. Let me just give you a preview of coming attractions. Did you know that, as you approach your closing, you have to have enough cash to cover such unexpected and surprise hits as appraisal fee, credit report fee, loan origination fee, loan "points," mortgage insurance application fee, assumption fee, reserves deposited with lender, title search and insurance, notary fees, bank's and your attorney's fees, adjustments, recording and transfer charges—had enough?

As soon as you decide you want to buy a house, make a trip to the library. There are several excellent books which can fill you in on specifics. These details (which would be a sure-fire sleeping pill now) will be engrossing reading when the realization hits you that you're going to have to live for many years in whatever house-buying decisions you make now.

A Better View of Buying Glasses and Contact Lenses

It's difficult to approach a purchase in the health care field in quite the same way you attack buying a refrigerator or car. You can always fix or exchange an appliance which is a lemon, but there are no guarantees—and very few replaceable parts—on your body, so you should give it the best. But, as we have learned, best is not always the most expensive.

You wouldn't trust a surgeon who advertised a super special one-week-only $99 appendix operation, and there is no need to respond to someone who brandishes a one-time-only, now-or-never, get-your-contact-lenses for only $20. The field of optometry and opthalmology is, nonetheless, a big business, and you should shop around. Get recommendations from your bespectacled friends and relatives after you take this peek at the optical field.

First, let's introduce the cast of characters in the eye-care arena. There are the three "O"'s. On one side of the ring we have the Opthalmologist, on the other we have the Optometrist. And then there is the Optician.

OPTHALMOLOGIST: An MD who does internship and residency specializing in surgery of the eyes and treatment of

Buying Glasses and Contact Lenses

eye diseases. Because he has that MD after his name, he charges more. (After all, he has to pay for his medical school.) It is a good idea, however, to choose an opthalmologist if you fear there is anything seriously wrong with your eyes.

OPTOMETRIST: A specialist who goes to optometry school for four years. The first two years are pretty similar to medical school. During the second two, he studies vision, perception, optics, lenses, etc. He is qualified to examine your eyes and prescribe glasses. If you don't already have your glasses prescription, an optometrist is probably the best bargain. He is obligated both legally and professionally to send you to an opthalmologist if he finds anything out of the ordinary.

OPTICIAN: Basically he's the guy who makes the glasses. He grinds lenses, puts them in the frames and adjusts them. He goes to optician's school for two years but cannot examine your eyes. You can save money by going to an optician only if you already have your glasses prescription from an opthalmologist or optometrist. (By law, you must be given your prescription when your eyes are examined.)

The choice begins to get a little complicated because some opthalmologists hire opticians in their offices to make glasses, and some opticians hire optometrists to examine eyes. But let's get on with how you can get good service from the specialist you choose.

When you call to make your appointment, ask how long the exam is. If it's anything under a half-hour, hang up and let your fingers do the walking to the next one on your list. In a good exam, your specialist should ask about your medical history. "Do you have any physical problems? Are you taking any medication," etc. Then he should have you read the chart to find out your visual acuity. Finally, he should make an internal eye exam with a special scope. By looking at your blood vessels and optic nerves, the opthalmologist or optometrist can see how healthy your eyes are. Then they check your eyes with lenses, and should test for glaucoma.

Some less reputable operations omit all but the lens test. Make sure you are given all of the other tests, as they are vital parts of eye care.

"What kind of lens shall I buy?" is the next big question. They are all pretty similar. Glass is heavier and scratches less, plastic is lighter and scratches more. There is hardly any variance in the quality of plastic and glass you'll buy. Most of the cost differentiation is in the frames—and the address of the specialist you go to. A prestige optometrist can give you little more than a responsible, less expensive one (other than some soft music and free coffee in his office).

"Shall I buy contact lenses?" This decision is based on a blend of cost, convenience, and vanity. If you decide yes, you ask yourself, "Hard lenses or soft?" Hard lenses are less expensive, last longer and can give better distance vision. They are also easier to handle and clean. Soft lenses are much easier to get used to.

It's always a good idea to determine what organizations your specialist belongs to. Most responsible professionals in the eye-care field belong to an organization like the American Optometric Association, the College of Optometrics and Vision Specialists or the American Academy of Opthalmologists. If you're taking your child for an exam, check that your specialist belongs to the Optometric Extension Program. This organization draws professionals who are especially interested in vision development.

One of the best reasons to ask about professional organizations is that it keeps your specialist on his toes for you. Once you mention an organization he respects enough to be a member of, he'll respect you more. He'll also subliminally realizes that, if you're not satisfied with his work, your recourse is to contact that organization.

Let me reprise my favorite tune for you yet again. When buying glasses or lenses, "Get All Your Guarantees in Writing." A little foresight in addition to your good glasses can help keep your eyes healthy a long, long time.

Protecting Your Home (and Pocketbook) with Homeowner's Insurance

Let's play a little game called "What's Wrong With This Sentence." The call is to an insurance agent. "Hello, this is Mr. Jones. I have a closing next Tuesday and I need some homeowner's insurance."

Answer to what's wrong with the above: EVERYTHING. And, yet, my insurance agent tells me, this is one of the most common approaches to purchasing homeowner's insurance. People need it quickly to get a mortgage, so they make a couple of calls and settle for whatever the agent decides to sell them. Like the housewife who feels the cake is her creation as long as she adds her fresh eggs to the mix, the consumer feels he's actually bought the best policy as long as he rolls his own on a few options. It's not that simple!

I'm practically convinced that insurance companies cram pack their policies with hundreds of complicated riders and floaters just to confuse you so you'll let the agent make most of the decisions for you and charge top dollar. For instance, here's the kind of minutiae many homeowners' policies deal with. If your dog bites a visitor, it's fully covered—*unless* it's a Doberman or German Shepherd. They're excluded. And, if your mutt decides to bite someone on more than one occasion, your whole policy can be cancelled because you did not keep

your dangerous dog restrained. Sounds ridiculous, but it's crucial stuff—if you happen to have a pooch.
There are a hundred "ifs" in each policy and there is no shorthand. The lengthy documents designed by actuaries and written by lawyers are often incomprehensible. So incomprehensible, in fact, that several states have passed laws saying the policies have to be written in plain English common usage. I'm afraid the only solution is going to be a time-consuming one. You must sit down with your agent. Ask for his computerized print-outs of coverage and discuss your options with him, making sure you understand. (The first time the majority of people read the fine print in their policies is when they are forced to look at it with bulging eyes and sweaty palms *after* an accident to see what was covered.)
There are, however, a few "no-no's" and a few "definitely-do's" that can save you a healthy amount on your premiums and a lot of heartache if something does happen to your home. We'll get into those in a few moments. But first let's start with your money-saving approach to this purchase.
You are going to do your initial shopping by phone, and, if you follow these tips, you are going to sound like you know all about your agent's business and, therefore, all about his prices. If you have never purchased homeowner's insurance before, you introduce yourself to the potential agent and tell him right up front:

WHERE THE HOUSE IS
HOW OLD THE HOUSE IS
   If the house is older than 1940, you must tell him whether or not the plumbing, heating and electricity have been updated.

IF THERE ARE FIRE HYDRANTS WITHIN 1000 FEET
HOW FAR THE NEAREST FIRE COMPANY IS
WHETHER THE HOUSE HAS CIRCUIT BREAKERS OR FUSES

Giving him the unsolicited answers to these last three questions is the winning combo for hinting that you're a real pro at buying insurance.

IF YOU HAVE SMOKE ALARMS, FIRE EXTINGUISHERS OR DEADBOLT LOCKS

These last tidbits of information can qualify you for substantial discounts on your premium. Depending on your policy, a simple $9.95 smoke alarm purchase could doubly pay for itself in the first year alone.

You should briefly describe the house, number of rooms, etc. and ask him for a price for x thousands of dollars coverage under "HOMEOWNER'S 2" (or HO 1, or HO 3).

Instead of using the giveaway novice's terms of "minimum," "moderate" or "complete" coverage, learn a few words of his lingo. Most agents will speak in terms of HOMEOWNER'S and then a number—Homeowner's 1, 2 or 3.

HO-1 (also called BASIC FORM)—Just protects you against wind, fire, burglars and vandals.

HO-2 (or BROAD FORM)—Adds such catastrophes as collapsing roofs, frozen pipes, falling objects and a few other more common hard knocks.

HO-3 (COMPREHENSIVE FORM)—Depending on the policy, includes just about every macabre destruction that the human mind could conjure except war.

Recommendation? Homeowner's 2 is a good bet and costs not much more than the basic form. But check it out. If you've always had a recurring nightmare that your Doberman was going to go mad and leap through your bay window, gnaw at the rugs and break all your antiques, you might sleep better with Homeowner's 3. Also, if HO 3 is just slightly more expensive than HO 2 in your area and situation, it does give broader coverage and should be considered.

If you have a favorite vase that you shudder to think might break or be stolen, you can buy a FLOATER just for that. Here's another fairly common vocabulary word that you should use either in the spirit of facilitating communication with your agent or not letting him know that you're an insurance neophyte over whose eyes wool can be pulled: RIDER. That's anything added to your policy, such as the "floater" above. If you're really rich, you should definitely consider an UMBRELLA policy to insure all liability losses above your regular insurance. It's usually not too expensive and will protect you against any vindictive guest who might slip, break a leg and get a lawyer to convince a judge that if he hadn't broken his leg he would have been the next Nureyev.

A real insider's question you should ask your agent—and a valuable one to know the answer to—is: "Which, if any, insurers do you have DRAFT AUTHORITY with?" Draft authority is granted to a company's preferred agents. They are actually given a checkbook from the insurer, and the agent can write out claim checks to his clients up to a certain amount. For you, that means almost instantaneous money for your claim.

If you have had homeowner's insurance before, your shopping task is much easier. You call various agents and simply read them the DECLARATION SHEET. That's the top page of your policy which specifies the coverage you had. The key phrase is, "Can you give me better coverage for less money?"

Even if you currently have home coverage that you're fairly happy with, the above is a good exercise. After you've checked with a few other agents for comparison, call your current agent and ask if he can improve your coverage or price. He'll look into it because he wants to keep those 20 percent renewal commissions coming in.

I'm going to leave all specific recommendations about which floaters and riders to add to your policy to you and your agent. There is only one crucial chunk of advice I want to offer. YOUR COVERAGE SHOULD BE FOR AT LEAST 80 PERCENT

OF THE REPLACEMENT COST OF YOUR HOME. Through some unbelievably convoluted and bizarre line of reasoning, insurers arrive at the conclusion that if your home is not insured for at least this, you'll only receive ⅝ of any loss or damage. Doesn't make sense to me (or my friendly agent), but that's the way it is.

As in auto insurance, not everybody can get the homeowner's insurance he wants, even if he's willing to pay for it. The major insurance companies have their prejudices too. For instance, some of them don't like smokers. (That I understand; more apt to start a fire.) They don't like live-togethers or "co-habitors." (You figure that one out. The only reason I can come up with is that they prefer to insure families that they can hit up for the big ticket later on—life insurance.)

And they're not going to be too receptive to selling insurance to convicted arsonists or radical arms-stockpilers. But you should have no trouble getting good coverage if you act like Mr. or Mrs. Middle America. Just be sure to give yourself enough time to shop around.

Legal Services for Less, or Often You Are Your Own Best Lawyer

There is only one proven way to cut down your legal costs—avoid lawyers! A lawyer, after four years of college, spends three arduous years learning all the ins and outs of getting exactly what he wants for his client. So how successful are you, the layman, going to be getting what you want (a good deal) against his getting what he wants (your money)?

There are, of course, many times when a lawyer is an absolute necessity—a native guide through our complex legal system. This chapter will help you determine when and if you need one, how to find the best one for the least amount of money, and how to be your own lawyer when you don't need one.

There are ways to resolve many matters without legal counsel. With a little standard legalese (taught here), you can make debtors and creditors break out in a cold sweat when they receive your document. A simple agreement written by you in legalese and stapled into a ten-cent "blue back" (bought in stationery stores) can often carry as much weight as a document produced by the most prestigious law firm. Through the use of standard legal forms sold in stationery stores for under a dollar, you can write a lease, incorporate a small business, draft a promissory note, write a simple will or transfer property within your family. Your own pen can be a mighty sword against rising legal costs in many routine situations where the inclination is to hire a lawyer.

WHEN YOU NEED A LAWYER

Before we roll up our sleeves and become do-it-yourselfers, let's tackle the problem of finding the right lawyer for the right price when you need one. If you have a substantial amount of assets or own a business of any size, you should have a good law firm to call upon. Having a big law firm behind you is analogous to having a good general practitioner family doctor, prepared to meet any and all emergencies. Practically every big burg in the U.S. has one leading law firm. The major cities, of course, have several. If your assets are substantial enough or your business sizeable enough—go with them. They cost a lot, but you're covered.

The rest of us common folk will want a lawyer only when we need one. And we want the best for the least. Here's how: Find out the name of the top firm—usually the biggest law firm in town. It's easy. Every schlock lawyer in the area will know the name of the biggie. He's either worked there, aspires to work there or is as mad as hell that he doesn't qualify for the job. Get the name from anyone in the legal community (or from a big directory called *Martindale Hubbell*, which I'll tell you about later) and call them. Explain what you want very concisely to the receptionist. Try to reduce it to one word like:

REAL ESTATE
TAX
LITIGATION (lawsuits)
ESTATE PLANNING (wills)
LABOR (the people working for you are giving you a hassle)
BANKRUPTCY (you know what that is)

CORPORATE (contracts and other business dealings and hassles)
PENSIONS

Say to the receptionist, I'd like to talk to an attorney in your _____ department. You fill in the blank from one of the words above. The receptionist will then almost assuredly put you through to whichever lawyer is available in that department. When he or she comes on the line, explain your problem succinctly and *ask the firm's hourly rate*. Chances are that at this top firm, it will be too high. Tell the lawyer that that is a bit steep and ask if there is a smaller, less expensive firm specializing in your type of need that he can recommend. Because you're talking to the biggest, they're not likely to be hungry for your smaller business. And unless you have a real stuffed-shirt on the line, he's going to tell you who to call. Thank him and hang up with the happy knowledge that you've been a smart detective and you now probably have the name of the very best lawyer for you.

Then call Mr. Right Lawyer and tell him that Mr. Unstuffed-Shirt at Biggie, Best and Brightest, Inc., suggested you contact him. It really is good to use a firm expert in your type of problem because even if their hourly rate is a bit higher than a tiny general-practice law firm's, a specialist is going to need to do less research and therefore spend less time coming up with the right way to deal with your situation.

There is another path you can traverse in your search for Mr. Right Lawyer. Doctors, teachers and shopkeepers don't go running around telling a reporter what they think of each other. But lawyers do; they tell the *Martindale Hubbell Law Directory*. This is a three-foot-wide set of books which reveals all. Every lawyer and law firm that's been around awhile is listed—and graded! In addition to all kinds of esoteric information about when the lawyer was born, where he was educated and even when he first passed the bar, they actually give him a score. The grade is A, B or C. C means "so-so" and A is tops. In addition, if the lawyer or firm is super-ethical, they give him a V, which stands for "very high ethical standards." If you get an A-V lawyer or law firm, you've got the best—at least according to the other barristers around town. You can get ahold of *Martindale Hubbell* at any library that has a law section.

Want a free lawyer? That's right, *free*. There are times, such as when you've been physically injured or have what you think may be a really good lawsuit, when the lawyer (or law firm) may work on spec. He or she may take your case on a *contingent fee* basis where you owe him ⅓ of the judgment if you win, but nothing (except basic expenses) if you lose. Ask Mr. Right Lawyer for a contingent fee, and if he agrees, you know what's next: Get it in writing and in detail.

If you can't get a contingent fee, understand that you will probably be charged by the hour, and that his hourly rate is usually not negotiable—and it would be meaningless even if it were. When you purchase a product, you can see, hold, and evaluate it. Even when you spend money on a doctor, you know how much time he or she spent with you, and you have some idea what was done for you. But most people have no idea what all those lawyer's "billable hours" are for. He could reduce his hourly wage and report greatly exaggerated billable hours.

Like any contracted help, the lawyer's fee is going to be based on his current workload, how much he wants/needs your case, and how much he thinks you can afford. Let him know that cost is a concern here. Ask him the following questions before retaining his services.

1.) "Where did you go to law school? What is your specialty? How many years have you practiced it? Where?" (This is enough on the personal. However, if you are insecure about the lawyer you are interviewing and want to risk being obnoxious, you could ask him if he made *Law Review*—a prestigious law school publication that the top 10 percent of law students get in. You could even ask his class standing, but reserve these last two questions for young lawyers that you really need to gain more confidence in before retaining.)

2.) "How many billable hours are required of Associates in your firm?" (Some firms require impossible quotas from their Associates and even Partners. If a firm demands over 35 *billable* hours per week, you are either going to have an exhausted barrister or an inflated bill.

3.) "Will you be giving me a monthly breakdown of what was done, how long it took and who in the firm did it?" (And then make sure you get it!)

4.) "Can you assure me that the rates won't change during the period of representation or litigation?"

5.) "How much does your firm charge for travel time or a day away from the office? How many hours constitute a day? If the trip is for more than one client, how do you bill it? Are lawyer's meals and entertainment charged to the client's account? Does the firm's personnel travel coach or first class?" (These questions will help convince the lawyer that you're pretty savvy about how law firms operate and will tend to make him warier of tacking extras onto your tab.) For the same reason, you can ask him how the duplication of documents in the office is charged, and if secretarial services are billed (they shouldn't be).

6.) A final very effective question is, "What are the hourly rates of the Partners, Associates and paralegals?" (Associates' should be from 50 to 75 percent of the Partners' rate. Paralegals' and law clerks' should be about one-third of a top Associate's billing rate.)

All legal fee arrangements should be in writing. No lawyer will be offended by this. "Put it in writing" is their most common utterance. He won't mind your asking. And, after you've asked all the questions above, he's going to respect you and know he's not dealing with the ordinary turkey.

A final note before going on to a crash course in avoiding a lot of legal costs—most contested legal fees are not collected. If your lawyer has overbilled or done what you consider to be an inept job, there is a sure-fire way to give him gooseflesh. Mention the disciplinary board. There is a good chance your case and tab will be reviewed. Don't just say "the disciplinary board," however. Show him you know what you're talking about. Find out from a court clerk at the county or state court (or the local bar association) what the disciplinary board for lawyers is in your state—it could be the Bar Association's Grievance Committee, the Lawyer Review Board or the Disciplinary Board of the State Supreme Court. Lawyers don't want to mess around with any of the above!

Keep in mind that there are middle-ground times when you don't need a really expert lawyer and yet you don't want to handle the situation yourself. Examples are uncontested divorces, being charged with driving under the influence of alcohol (called DWI or DUI) and simple bankruptcy. In these cases, simply check the Yellow Pages or even the classified section of the newspaper. Lawyers are now allowed to advertise and they even put package prices on the above in the newspaper. Call around. You may get an old goat who sounds like he's under the influence himself or a young hotshot who's just starting. Actually, what I'm saying here is you may get anything. So call around until you like the sound of the lawyer and then get a solid price and pay him a visit.

DO IT YOURSELF DEPARTMENT

There is a movement underfoot in this country to stamp out our tremendous dependence on lawyers and help the public perform certain simple legal actions themselves. There is is a company in California called "Nolo Press" and they publish a lot of do-it-yourself lawyer type books. They are excellent if you are declaring bankruptcy, want to authorize someone to act on your behalf by giving them a power of attorney, are considering suing someone in small claims court or a myriad of other simple legal transactions. They even have a "living together" kit that helps "roommates" to do things like purchase property together and be protected. Being in Berkeley, they have, naturally, a book on how to protect the computer software programs you write and a gay/lesbian couples legal handbook! If you have a legal matter that you think you can handle yourself, check your library or bookstore or drop them a line at 950 Parker Street, Berkeley, CA, 94710.

Another little-known legal gem is called "Blumberg's Legal Forms." They or other legal forms can be found in most major stationery stores. Mr. Blumberg publishes hundreds of forms for use by lawyers and laymen alike. If you're renting a house, apartment or office space, he has standard leases. If you're incorporating a small business, he has standard forms. He has power of attorney forms, blank affidavits, bills of sale for cars and boats, promissory notes, and lots more. Knowing how sue-happy people (especially lawyers) are becoming, to be on the safe side, Mr. Blumberg invoked the lawyer's favorite phrase, "C.Y.A." The first two words are "cover" and "your." He warns that it might be problematic for the average consumer to use some of his forms. Fair enough, but, from my experience, these and other standard legal forms are tremendous money savers for *simple* legalities.

Millions of hard-earned dollars are spent each year on lawyers' fees for writing simple contracts and threatening letters—two easy things you can effectively do yourself. Suppose you want to make an agreement with someone else on just about anything. Let's say you want your kids to use your next door neighbor's swimming pool and she's agreeable to that as long as you wouldn't sue if anything happened. Or perhaps you and your neighbor want to start a small part-time cookie-selling business out of your kitchen. Suppose anything! You'll need an agreement, but, if it's small time, not a lawyer. Here's how to write an agreement that will cover that anything.

As an example, let us enter the world of not-so-high finance for a moment. We'll choose a business many of us have been in—albeit a few years ago. Suppose you and your friend, Suzie Smith, want to open a lemonade stand together. You want to make sure that all expenses come off the top, that you split the profits 50/50 and that she doesn't go and open her own lemonade stand without you once your joint stand becomes successful. The parts italicized below are standard for all contracts. We'll call it the "Agreement–Witnesseth––Whereas–Whereas–Now Therefore" for short. Here we go:

AGREEMENT

This Agreement is made on this (insert date) by and between Suzie Smith, (hereinafter, Suzie), an individual residing at 129 Main Street, Anytown, USA, and Betsy Jones (hereinafter B.J.), an individual residing at 131 Main Street, Anytown, USA.

WITNESSETH:

WHEREAS, Suzie Smith wishes to open a lemonade stand with Betsy Jones; *and*

WHEREAS, Betsy Jones agrees to open a lemonade stand with Suzie Smith;

NOW, THEREFORE, in consideration of the foregoing premises and the mutual benefit to be derived by the parties hereto from the observance of the covenants, conditions, and agreements contained herein, the parties hereto hereby agree as follows:

Then you put in all your agreements about profit split and no competition in plain English. Simply number your agreements, put a signature line for both, and presto—thanks to the old "Agreement–Witnesseth–Whereas–Whereas–Now Therefore" format, Suzie and you feel legally bound and no lawyer is any richer.

Let me give you the solution to some other common problems we are constantly faced with. The solution is the "lawyer's letter" sans a lawyer. We'll call it the "Big Scare Letter" and it works in all kinds of situations. It's heavy artillery. Use it and watch debtors pay, creditors abandon their charges and people whom you find a nuisance immediately drop their objectionable ways and comply with your demands. It is a form of a lawyer's threatening letter that has litterally saved me thousands of dollars in the past few years. This "Big Scare" letter has never failed to work for me on unscrupulous car repair garages and other vendors.

Start with plain white 8½" × 11" (or better yet, 8½" by 14" if you can find it) paper. Never use paper with a letterhead, and always *type* your Big Scare letter. Here's the form. The capitalized parts always stay the same. All you need to do is fill in the facts.

NOTICE

Centered at the top of the page, this is shorthand for "Look out, Buddy, this is serious stuff."

IN THE MATTER OF

This officializes the situation into a legal "matter." You must caption your matter with the person's or company's name whom you are confronting. For example, "In the matter of John Doe, individually and as a respresentative of John Doe Enterprises, Inc."

Name of addressee   DATE OF MAILING
Mailing address   (date here)1
City, State, zip code

NOTICE OF

You've got some choices here. One of the most common is "Notice of Tortious Fraud." This can be used for stores who have overcharged you or given you a faulty product, or for professionals who have overcharged, failed to perform properly or misrepresented their services. If you are directing your Big Scare letter toward someone who is annoying you, it is "Notice to Abate Actionable Nuisance."

STATEMENT OF COMPLAINT

Here you outline your gripe—but, no matter how filled with ire you are, you must sound totally dispassionate. Dispassion is the lawyer's trademark. Organize your thoughts and list the points of your case. It's often a good idea to put them in consecutively numbered sequence. This helps clarify your thinking.

DEMAND FOR ACTION

Here's where you tell the sucker what you want him to do—replace his product, reduce the cost, pay up, keep his kids out of the pool—whatever you want. Just make sure that your demand is reasonable, and set a time limit for it. Don't permit any room for his procrastination.

ULTIMATUM

We all know what that means. It's what your going to do if he doesn't right his wrong. This paragraph can be pretty standard legalese. My favorite: "In the event you fail to respond to my demand, I shall seek legal counsel with the intention of commencing a civil action against you for fraud. I shall seek a verdict large enough to encompass both compensatory damages and punitive damages based on your fraud and misrepresentations. This may be substantial."

The last thing under Ultimatum is: "Copies of this correspondence and other relevant documents will be sent to:" And here you list everybody you can think of—the Department of Consumer Affairs, Office of the Attorney General, Consumer Frauds Bureau, State Consumer Protection Board, Better Business Bureau, the local Chamber of Commerce—anybody and everybody you think might be of concern to the recipient. Include their addresses to show how serious you are.

(Your signature)
YOUR NAME

Mailing address
City, State, zip code

Certified Mail No. (number here)

   Armed with this knowledge of how to word a simple contract and how to write a lawyerly scare letter plus knowing what books and forms to turn to for specific legal needs, you're in great shape. Now here's my C.Y.A. If you don't think you can handle the situation by yourself, go back to the beginning of this chapter and re-read how to find the best and cheapest lawyer for you and, once found, how to keep him on his toes.

Getting the Best Paint Job— and the Best Price

On the subject of painting (houses and apartments, not masterpieces on canvas), my very own painter, Harry Gateman, is our guru. And to quote Harry:

"Sure, you gotta know how to talk to a painter. Not me, but a lotta other guys—the unscrupulous ones—they're gonna try to get whatever they can. It's only human nature. Especially if you're a woman and you deal with them smart, like I'm gonna tell you how, their hair will stand on its end. They'll say, 'Hey, this is no babe in the woods—I better deal straight.'"

O.K. Harry, how do you deal with them smart?

"Well, first of all, it's who makes the call. Say you live in an apartment. You're entitled to a new paint job once every three years. And say it's between times but you want a little fancying up on the place. You don't make the call. Have your landlord give the painter a jingle. Landlords always get a *much* better price because of the volume. I don't get rich on landlord's jobs but it keeps my men busy and I make a few bucks on the extras. Same thing if you've got a house. Get your agent to call, because I figure, 'Hey, maybe we get in good with him and he'll give us a lot of work.' So what I'm basically saying is, I'm gonna give those guys a better price than I'm gonna give you."

Getting the Best Paint Job

Harry went on to say that if it's difficult to arrange for your agent or landlord to get a price, "play the estimate game. "Call the painter up and say, 'Look, I got a six-room house and I want an estimate.' When you see him, you say, 'I hope you can come in low because you were highly recommended, but I gotta get three estimates.' Bang, right away, that'll put him on his toes and make him aware that he better be competitive if he wants the job. He won't balk—that's standard in the industry."

My painter's next suggestion obtains when dealing with any contractor.

"The reason you get three estimates is because it's good to get two people who are in agreement. It's just like going to three doctors. 'Cause the way I would feel about it if I was a layman—if one guy wanted half of what the other one wanted, I'd feel, 'Gee, maybe this guy who wants half doesn't know what the hell he's doin' and could really louse up the place. He doesn't know the business. Who needs 'em?' Whereas you get two cheap ones, you figure the fancy priced one is a ripoff."

It almost goes without saying, but get a written estimate detailing everything—kind of paint, number of coats, drop cloths to protect floors and furniture. In architect's specifications, it says the job will be done "properly," not just "in a workmanlike fashion." Make sure "done properly" is in your contract. Here's a hint. Compare all three written estimates. Learn what can be done from the two you are not choosing. Then make sure all points are covered in the estimate of the painter you do select. Keep in mind that any good painter knows from looking at a job how many hours of scraping and spackling are necessary, so do not let him say he'll charge by the hour and let you know when it's done. Solidify a price before he starts. Usual payment terms for a job are a "third, a third and a third." That is a third as down payment, a third in the middle of the job and the final third upon completion.

Harry continues:

"Then you show him you got smarts about the business, so you can really talk him down."

O.K., how? "Suppose the walls are in pretty good condition. You say, 'Look, it needs very little PREPPING—you're not going to have to spend much time SCRAPING AND SPACKLING. It's a clean paint job.' Right away he knows you know what the most time consuming thing for him is (prepping)—and therefore, his biggest mark-up item."

Harry went on to say that if there is a lot of prepping, you can always point out some of the other money-saving features of your particular job. A painter's expense is in time and paint. Colors "off the shelf" cost considerably less than custom colors which have to be blended at the shop. So, bring it to his attention if you're using a standard color. In apartments, a painter is entitled to charge more for a color. But if the whole room is the same color—a standard color—make him aware that you know it costs him no more than basic white.

One of the reasons a painter charges more for a color is that often the customer wants the ceiling white and it is time-consuming for him to make the break. His little buzz word for that is CUTTING IN a color. If your room is all one color, tell him there is no cutting in, so the job should go pretty quickly.

Harry's advice on this:

"One bad negotiating technique that the dummies use is: 'But you don't have to paint that wall, it's got wallpaper on it.' Dumb, dumb, dumb! Then I hit them with how much more trouble it is for me to cut in around the wall paper. When somebody steps into that trap, I tell 'em, 'You better quit while you're ahead. You keep pointing things like that out to me and I'll charge more.'"

A good insider's question that you should ask your prospective painter as you're pointing to a rough spot on the wall: "Are you going to SPOT PRIME this?" Spot priming is putting primer sealer over the spackling for a smooth finish.

"Once the guy's given you the estimate, always use the old bargaining routine. Say something like, 'Is that the best you can do,' or 'Can't you do any better?' Painters always cover their rumps and can always move a bit on the price. Look, you don't ask, you don't get. You might say to a $1700 job, 'Look I'd like to use you, but I got another estimate for $1500. Can't you match that?' Usually in that case, I'll say, 'Sure, meet me in the middle" and I'll do it for sixteen. So you save a hundred. Better in your pocket than his, right?

"But do meet him in the middle. Don't be a pig or you might end up robbing yourself. If he goes too low and gets ticked off, he might mess you up by pulling some cheap tricks that the unscrupulous guys use."

Like what?

"Well, they might go out to Jersey and buy some bulk cheap paint that's not worth the can it's in, and then they put Benjamin Moore (reputed to be the best indoor paint) labels on it so you think you're getting the good stuff. Or they might thin the paint down with water or paint thinner. You can't tell if they do that from just looking at the wall, but when you try to wash it, the paint'll come off on your rag. Or they might try to get away with fewer coats than you contracted for."

How can you guard against things like that?

"Well, first of all, don't rip his pants off. Let him have a square deal so he doesn't have to cut corners. Then, keep an eye on 'em. Try to stay around while they're working. One of the tricks I use with my men is, after I get the job started, I say 'Look, I may see you around two.' I have no intention of coming back, but it keeps 'em on their toes. It's good if they think the customer could walk in any minute.

"Also, tell 'em you'd like to see the paint sealed in the cans before they start and to submit receipts for the paint to you. A lotta people ask me that because there are a lotta guys in the business who make it bad for the legitimate ones."

Armed with the above, you'll probably get the best possible deal your painter can offer you. It's really throwing perfume on the violet to use the following on your painter, but it's irresistible. As you're walking out one morning, say over your shoulder, "Don't leave any HOLIDAYS." Holidays is an industry-wide term meaning "undone spots" or "spots not covered well." Architects' specifications of a job designate "No holidays."

Getting a Good Deal on Car Repair Good Luck!

"I'd be hard pressed to find a totally honest car-repair facility in the country today." This is a direct quote from a high executive of the National Highway Traffic Safety Administration. And, unless you have had some unusual luck in this area, you'd probably agree with him. I have spent thousands of dollars for faulty repairs and the replacing of perfectly good parts on my car. I have paid exorbitant labor costs for the hours that mechanics spent shooting the breeze instead of trouble shooting.

How can you get a better deal from your car repair shop? It's tough! But it can be done. Take a little knowledge for ammunition, and prepare to do battle.

There are, obviously, two things that you pay for—labor and parts. Although often ignored, there are books that almost every repair shop has which regulate both. Almost every garage has a giant-size greasy book lying around called "the labor manual." There are different publishers but all are basically similar. Every possible repair on almost every type of car is listed, with the amount of time it should take one mechanic to make that repair.

The other dog-eared books on repair shop's shelves are various parts books listing manufacturers and prices. There are vastly differing categories of prices. You'll find:

LIST PRICE—Top dollar. The man off the street pays this.
DEALER or USER PRICE—Your local garage probably pays this.
JOBBER PRICE—Best deal. Wholesalers and big facilities pay this tab.

What you pay to the shop is the list price, or sometimes even higher if you don't peek at the book over your mechanic's shoulder and haggle a bit. Your shop pays either the Dealer or User Price and pockets the difference as hidden profit. Keep in mind that the list price is usually 25 to 35 percent above the dealer/user price. Don't get too concerned with the jobber price. That's about 40 percent below list and only for big operators who buy in bulk.

Although few customers ask, they are permitted to look at the books and to check the prices. If you know what's wrong with your car, ask the shop to let you look at the parts manual. Then look up the part you need. There might be several different manufacturers of a particular part, so discuss which one is the cheapest that will do the job. The mechanic will probably give you a price range for the part. After he does that, act like that is a bit too expensive and ask if a rebuilt part (always cheaper) will do the job just as well. There's a good chance it will.

After you've determined what part you want, and whether it's new or rebuilt, you will want to get an exact price for the job before you leave your ailing auto in his hands. If the mechanic doesn't have the part in stock, ask him to call his supplier *while you wait*. When he hangs up the phone, he'll give you the "list" price. You can then ask him if he gets the price at "dealer" or "user." If he gets user price, ask him if he can

A Good Deal on Car Repair

do any better than "list" for you. Whether he can or not, at least he will know that you are aware of the difference. And, as in any successful haggling, the more the seller thinks you know, the more apt he is to be fair with you.

By the way, make sure that the garage is prepared to do all the work on your car. If they have to subcontract, their markup comes out of your pocket.

Once you've agreed on the price of the parts you need, ask the mechanic to save your old part and the box the new one comes in for you. Then you ask to look at "the labor manual." Every conceivable auto repair job is listed in this publication, with how long the job should take to complete. An honest mechanic will go by the book rather than how long the job actually takes. If he finishes your job in a shorter time than the labor manual decrees, he comes out ahead. If it takes longer, he should not pass the cost on to you. Look at the labor manual, see how long the repair should take, and then, instead of the mechanic giving you a price, you and he determine the price together. His hourly labor fee should be posted.

An added precaution is this. Once you've left the shop, you might want to call your car dealer or a parts supplier yourself and confirm the price of the part you're buying. If it's lower than the list price the mechanic quoted, call him and tell him the "good news"—that you were able to find that exact same part at a better price. He'll have no argument for giving you the part at his exaggerated price.

It's akin to bringing your own eggs to a restaurant and asking the chef to make an omelette for you, but if you establish a good working relationship with a particular repair shop, you might be permitted to pick up the part yourself from a parts house and deliver it to the mechanic. Check the Yellow Pages. Some parts houses have no qualms about giving retail customers the dealer price. A big ad will usually jump out at you which brandishes their "discount" prices. Call a regular parts house for comparison, on an alternator for example, to determine if bona fide discounts are offered. If a discount parts house checks out, keep their number on a solid gold rolodex card. Use it whenever you need parts.

If you don't know what the trouble with your car is, you leave yourself open to one of the most surreptitious ways that an unscrupulous garage jacks up the price. This is false diagnosis—you pay a lot for a repair that isn't done (or even that your car doesn't need) in addition to paying for the fixing of the real problem. Be on the lookout when you are told your auto has two infirmities. One remedy for this is to stay with the car while the mechanic makes the repair. However, in some larger repair facilities, this is not possible and is potentially time-consuming.

Another major rip-off (traditionally used on women and those inexperienced in a car's mechanical function) is to charge labor for searching for the problem. You should not have to pay for diagnosis of a common problem (except if it is done by machine). Any reputable repair shop will give free estimates including a diagnosis. Here's a pennywise tip. Don't hesitate to get several estimates in writing. Make sure that they agree on the problem and then choose the one with the best price.

If your car has one of those dreaded mystery diseases and you are told that they cannot find the problem easily and must charge you labor, tell them to stop if they get to one hour and call you for your "keep-a-goin' or quit-now" decision. At least they'll know you're counting the sand grains as they fall through the hourglass.

It is by far better to know the specific illness your car suffers from when you take it to the repair shop. Look in the owner's manual and see if you can figure out the problem. Even mentioning a few possible problems to the garage indicates that you know a little bit about cars. And, of course, highlight the cheapest one.

One sure-fire money saver is to have a friend who is a mechanic. If you don't know any mechanics, try to find one who will moonlight for you. Finding a good one who will do the work is a good way to circumvent the shop's markup. Even if your mechanic isn't set up to make repairs in the moonlight, have him diagnose your car's problem. You can then call around to different garages and find out how much they will charge to make that repair. Needless to say, prices differ vastly.

If you can get your friend the mechanic to make the call to the garage, he'll probably get a better price just because he knows what he's talking about. Try to talk him into it—especially if you're a woman. Sad but true, car repair is one of the most male chauvinistic fields there is. Ladies, I hate giving this advice, but unless you are very sure of yourself, have your sons, fathers, boyfriends, grandfathers—any male—take your car to the shop to negotiate price.

When you pick up your car after it's been fixed, have the mechanic show you what he did. Make sure he gives you your old parts back and shows you the box the new part came in. If you have requested a rebuilt part and the mechanic has to keep your part for trade-in, at least look at it. Then ask for the guarantee to be written on your bill.

Last but by no means least, if it is permitted, pay by credit card. You're in good shape if you paid with your plastic. If the problem persists or you are otherwise dissatisfied with the repair, don't pay the garage's bill on your credit card. This way the garage has to give you satisfaction or you don't pay.

Nobody likes to be tattled on and garages are no exception. Some of them live in fear of being reported to the various organizations of which they are members. Enough complaints and they could lose all the benefits that come from their membership. One of the strongest organizations monitoring garages is the AAA—The American Automobile Club. It is almost worthwhile choosing a repair shop because it's an AAA franchise. In order for a facility to become AAA approved, it has to meet certain criteria in manpower, facility appearance, equipment, customer service and community reputation. The AAA doesn't fool around. They conduct an investigation of the facilities and then a review board decides to grant or not grant approval. The garages then must sign a contract which basically guarantees their workmanship. If you're not happy with their work you contact the AAA and they'll look into it for you. The garage has to agree with the AAA's arbitration.

If you don't like paying towing charges, walking to garages with an empty gas can, giving away your money to a locksmith every time you leave your keys in the locked car, and paying trucks to pull you out of ditches, you should probably join the AAA. The average $30 per year membership gets you all free minor repairs that don't have to be done in a garage. I hope the AAA folk don't see this book or they might revoke my membership when they read that my heap of a car received at least $500 worth of free towing and on-the-road repairs last year alone.

One last thought. Should you even repair your car once it takes on jalopy status? There's a tried-n-true formula that might help you with your decision. Find out the book value of your car. We'll call it "BV." Then get the average of a couple of repair estimates ("RE"). Divide the repair estimate by the book value and get the replacement percentage ("RP"). So RE divided by BV = RP. Got it? If RP is 25 percent or less, repair. If RP is 40 percent or more, replace. Between 25 and 40, it's your move.

Cutting Your Printing Costs Up to 90 Percent

Want to learn a magic trick that turns one hour and four dollars into a four-hundred-dollar job that'll only cost you forty bucks? All you need is a little cardboard, a jar of rubber cement, some scissors and maybe a blue pencil.

The next time you want personal stationery or a flier for your club's annual event, don't go running to the stationery counter of a big department store or hire an artist. For some reason the growing cadre of American do-it-yourselfers has not discovered the tremendous savings in printing costs that they can realize.

Printing isn't just for businesses. Even if you are a full-time homemaker, I guarantee that sooner or later you are going to want something printed. The secret lies in giving your printer a finished copy of what you want so he can work from that. In the business it's called a CAMERA READY MECHANICAL, and we're going to teach you how to make one. You'll also learn how to get the best paper inexpensively, and how to choose which printing process is best and cheapest for your project. It may be a little bewildering, but, if you follow this chapter closely, you can save up to 90 percent on your next printing job.

As an example, let's say that you are the one faced with the task of putting together a little flier to spread the word about your club's annual Swine Fest (no joke—pig-eating parties are big doings in some parts of the South). You've decided you want a four-page flier with a large headline on the front page saying "Y'ALL COME!" On the second page you want a drawing of a fat and happy pig with an apple in his mouth. On the third, you want, in fairly large type, all the details of the pig-out. And on the last page, you feel there should be some history of the time-honored tradition of pig devouring, and some information on just how one can join your exclusive club.

Now that you've rolled up your sleeves and decided to save $360 dollars on this job, you have several questions to answer.

1.) How are you going to get the headlines, artwork and type done?
2.) How are you going to lay it out? (In other words, how are you going to place it on your "mechanical" so the printer can reproduce it? A "mechanical" is a mock-up of what you want reproduced.)
3.) What paper are you going to have it printed on?
4.) How are you going to get it reproduced?

Let's start at the end. There are basically three ways to get your flier reproduced. First there is XEROX—we all know what that is. If you just need a few, say up to a hundred, and you're not that worried about quality, this is the best bet. The good news is that you can get your flier in black type on a myriad of colored backgrounds for pennies a copy. The bad news is that the quality is very irregular. Some will be lighter, some will be darker, and there can be "snow" or spots on your work depending on the machine's mood of the moment. Photos do not come out well with Xerox, but line drawings are fine. If this is your choice, you go to a Xerox shop. They can probably do a hundred while you wait.

Next step up is OFFSET—a photographic process. A camera picture is taken of your work and then is printed. Offset is the choice for over 100 pieces if you have no photographs that have to come out well. You can get a nice variety in color here, because in the larger shops you can ask for colored ink and have it offset on any color paper at a small extra charge. Check with the offset man to make sure that you've chosen colors with enough contrast to be readable. The quality is much finer, because every one is exactly the same and the sketch of your pig will come out exactly as drawn. Most printers do offset, as do the larger Xerox establishments.

Finally, there is LETTERPRESS or the full printing process. The quality is excellent, but the printer has to make a metal plate—an expensive process. If you have any colors or photos that have to come out well, this is your only choice. But for a simple flier such as we're discussing, it would not be necessary. If you are going to have the same flier or brochure printed many times, or for an extremely large number of pieces (BIG RUNS), this could be the ticket. The first 1000 are the most expensive. The price drops as you print more. This is because, after the plate is made, all you're paying for is the paper, a man watching to see that the very fast printing machine doesn't go haywire, and a few pennies in ink. (When you pick up your order, keep the plate so you won't have to go to the expense in your next printing.) Many print shops do all three—letterpress, offset and Xerox.

Now, let's consider your headline. You can have "Y'all Come!" TYPESET, hand drawn, word processed, or a fourth choice called TRANSFER LETTERING. Typesetting is the most expensive of the four, but the most professional-looking. You have a large selection of TYPEFACES (types of print) and you can choose from many sizes. The size of the type in typesetting is measured in POINTS. Point sizes at most shops range from 2 or 3 (very small, almost unreadable type that insurance companies and auto dealers use in their contracts) to 72 points—as in a big headline. Regular typewriting size is 10 to

12 points. If you want this variety and professionalism you can have everything in your flier typeset (except the pig, of course). It is expensive but it looks great. A middle choice might be to have just the headline and the date, time, and place of the swine-fest typeset. (For the headline, you could even take a black pen or magic marker and just draw "Y'all Come" in whimsical letters). But unless you have a touch of the artist in you, the job could look pretty tacky. The rest of the information (called COPY) could be typed by you on a typewriter that gives a good, clean impression. "Copy" is the word they use for any writing—the headlines and smaller print.

A less expensive and more viable alternative to typesetting is word processing. Word processing shops are sprouting up all over the country. The drawback is that they do not have the variety of typefaces. Nor is there the sharpness and clarity of typesetting. You might want to look at their work, however. BODY copy usually refers to a lot of words like regular typewriting. If you have access to a good typewriter, the body copy can simply be typed and reproduced with no problem. If you have the typing reduced in size just slightly, it looks almost like typeset copy.

Your printer can have whatever copy you like typeset for you, but here's a word to the wise. He charges about a 25 percent markup because he probably has it sent it out to a typesetter. Eliminate the middle man. Look in the Yellow Pages and find an ad for typesetting or word processing. Go there yourself and have the copy set. Then take it CAMERA READY to your printer or offset man.

Keep in mind that prices in supposedly "to the trade" shops are much cheaper. Find out who in your town does typesetting for businesses and go directly there. Just like your printer, the typesetter will show you various typefaces which will come in different point sizes.

The real big savers who don't mind a little handiwork can do the following for their headlines. Buy something called

TRANFER LETTERING. The most popular brands are "Letraset" and "Presstype," which come in a great variety of typefaces and can be found in art stores and big stationery shops. These are acetate sheets with several of each letter of the alphabet and a selection of numbers on them. In essence, you are about to do your own "typesetting." Get a good piece of white paper. You hold the letter you want imprinted over the paper and rub with a little stick—and the letter comes out in bold black type on your paper. Then you repeat for each letter you want. You cut this out and, if you have a steady hand and good eye, you paste this in the right position on a piece of white cardboard and you have created your own CAMERA READY MECHANICAL.

Providing the printer with a camera ready mechanical means that he does not have to do any typesetting, cutting or pasting for you. You have provided him with a mock-up of exactly what you want reproduced. It is by far the cheapest way to do it. It involves your buying a piece of white cardboard, the same size or slightly larger than what you want printed. (We'll use the word "printed" here to cover Xeroxed, offset or letterpressed.) You take your headline, the drawing of the pig and all your other copy and you paste it in exactly the position you want. Rubber cement is best because it sticks in position fast but is moveable until it dries. If you have any directions for the printer (like how far from the edge of the paper you want the copy to start), you can write right on the cardboard with an inexpensive little pencil called a REPRO pencil. It is a pencil with a blue lead that will not show up in any photographic printing process. When everything is in position on the cardboard, you have created what the artists call a MECHANICAL. The mechanical is the result of your cut 'n' paste job—it's the camera ready product.

To get a better idea of what the finished flier will look like, the pros paste a piece of onion skin or tissue thin paper over the mechanical. They tape it only across the top. When you look through it, you see only the black type showing through.

Then you give the mechanical to your printer, and all he can charge you for is the printing process. It definitely pays.

The next thing to consider for your pig-fest flier is size. When you're having a flier or brochure printed, the trick is to avoid too many cuts, and get as many pieces as possible out of the large sheet it's printed on. Most printers easily handle up to 11" × 17". After that, they need a very expensive press. If your work needs to be done on that, you're going to help pay for their press. Try to keep your sizes divisible into the standard 8½" × 11" or 11" × 17" to avoid extra cutting or trimming charges. For instance a 4¼" × 5½" would be less expensive than a 5" × 6" because you could only get one of the latter out of each 8½" × 11" and there would be extra cutting charges.

Let's choose 4¼" × 5½" for our flier. That gives us two per 8½" × 11" sheet of paper. It's called "running two up." Can you figure out why?

Turn to page two of the flier—the pig. Several choices here. First, you can draw, or have an artist friend draw, the pig. You'll cut your costs considerably if you keep it black-and-white—what is called a simple LINE DRAWING. If you get into grays, you'll have to resort to what is called SCREENING, which adds to your tab. Another final note on getting your porker printed—Letraset or Presstype can come to the rescue here too. Ask for their animal selection. Or, look through books of drawings. You can Xerox a good-looking pig and paste him right on your mechanical and the drawing will be treated just like copy for printing purposes.

SCREENING is a process that you might want to consider if you'd like a little color. It's a lot cheaper than several colors. It involves using a colored ink, and is a "separating the dots" process which makes the ink lighter or darker. If you need a color in your brochure, ask your printer about the screening process. Deep reds can be contrasted with a soft pink through the screening process and you're only paying for one color.

Cutting Your Printing Costs

I'm only going to say one thing about color here: It *greatly* increases your cost each time you add a color. You get your printer involved in what he calls "color separations," which means running your job through the press for each color and washing down the press before and after each new color—a time consuming and messy process. If you really want the apple in your pig's mouth to be red, you can have the kids sit around the kitchen table and fill it in with red magic markers after your flier's printed. Sometimes a small accent of color is even more striking than an expensive full-color job.

Certain printers are like so many other business people: The more you know, the less they charge. The most common blooper that gives the novice away is for him to bring in a color photo and say he wants it in his inexpensive little flier. Forget it! The average mug shot demands a lot of colors—a lot of color separations, a lot of washing the press, and therefore Big Money.

Another printing technique we'll only touch on lightly here is reproducing a black-and-white photograph. If you have to have a smiling photograph of the proud winner of last year's hog-eating contest in your brochure, your printer will tell you there will be a charge for the HALFTONE. Even if you don't know exactly what you're talking about, say to him, "Oh, a good VELOX will suffice," and you'll save about ⅔ of the halftone cost. So you'll know what you're talking about, briefly, "halftone" is top of the line photo reproduction and "velox" is a "separating the dots" process like that used in the newspapers. If you take a magnifying glass to newspaper photos, you'll see that they are made up of thousands of little dots—a velox process that is sufficient for all but the top quality printing jobs.

Last thing you should know before you leave the novice category and become an "Intermediate in Good Standing" is what a PHOTOSTAT is. It's a camera reproduction—a nice clean sharp copy of print or a drawing. It comes in real handy because it can be enlarged or reduced whatever percentage you like for your "mechanical." It's another economy move to look up "photostats" in the Yellow Pages and get your reduction or enlargement there rather than pay the printer's markup.

Let me here give you a cursory crash course in choosing paper for stationery, fliers, brochures or anything else.

You can buy your paper from the printer or, especially if you live in a big town, you can go to a paper house and pick out your own, thus avoiding the printer's markup. These places don't usually like to sell small retail orders, so when you walk through their door, know exactly what you want and how much. Do a little pre-shopping by looking at samples at a stationery store. Paper is described by finish, rag content and weight. Just a few examples of finish are: "cockle" (a wavy finish), "laid" (if you hold it up to the light, you see vertical lines) or "wove" (smooth).

Usually the higher the rag content, the higher the price. One hundred percent rag is very fine, 20 percent rag is plain bond. Then there is a top-of-the-line paper called Strathmore, which is 100 percent cotton. So you really have to do a little feeling of the paper to zero in on what to ask for at the paper house. Paper is also described by weight. Nine pound is onion skin, 16 is very light, 20 is your everyday white bond, and on up. Anything over 80 becomes "card stock." If you're supplying your own paper, give the printer some overage. There's a 2 percent mistake margin that is perfectly normal.

Let's talk about stationery for a moment. It's nice to have your own stationery, but personalized stationery ordered through those pretty books in fine department or stationery stores costs approximately 25 percent more than if you get it from your printer. And, because you now have enough graphic artist's knowledge (the kind of artist who specializes in what we're talking about) to do your own mechanical, you'll wind up paying *much* less. You use the same process to create your own stationery as the swine-fest promoter used in his flier. Get a piece of white cardboard the same size (or slightly larger) than your desired stationery. Then go to either your printer or typesetter and choose a type style (called TYPEFACE), a type size (again, in POINTS) from his book. Choose one for the face of the stationery and one for the envelope.

Once again, steady-handed penny watchers, choose the presstype style you like and do-it-yourself. Then paste this copy on the cardboard in the position you want it. Mark where the corners of your stationery will be with your "repro" pencil. This time you have created your own "camera ready mechanical" for your stationery.

Take that with the copy for the envelope to the printer. For the envelope, simply give your printer the typeset address and tell him where you want it on the envelope. That's easy for him, so usually there's no great saving in creating your own envelope mechanical. You can choose a paper and ink color right there from his book, and you've paid a fraction of what the department store would charge you.

After writing this, I priced the pig-out flier with several graphic artists. Most of them were in the $400 ballpark. Choosing transfer lettering for the headlines, clean typing for the body copy, a book photo for piggy, and offset for printing, the job came to 500 fliers for under $40. Sheer money magic!

Getting a Fair Shake from Ma Bell

Today, over 400 million phone calls will be made. Of those 400 million calls, there will be an astronomical number overcharged by phone companies, and millions of frustrated callers unable to communicate their needs to the operators. Untold thousands of people called by telephone solicitors will purchase non-existent or valueless goods. Long distance services are sprouting up like wildflowers—and with as much variety. Each has a different price structure and list of services. To add to the chaos, there are dozens of fabulous features that the telephone folk won't advertise because they don't make money on them. You can be losing money right now because you didn't know enough to ask for them.

So all this is going to be cleared up in one chapter of this book? Highly doubtful. But I can almost guarantee that, by turning your concentration for a moment on that jingling apparatus in your home or office, you will save big bucks on your phone bill.

The patent for the little tool used daily by almost every American was granted on March 7, 1876, to, you guessed it, Alexander Graham Bell. The phone has come a long way, baby, in a little over a hundred years—but it has a lot further to go before we're paying what we should, and getting the results we want from it.

A Fair Shake from Ma Bell

The next time you have a hankering for a little light reading, take a look at the first five to ten pages of your phone book. It's brimming with information on how you can play the Saving-Money-On-Your-Phone game. The specifics vary from state to state, even from community to community, but let me give you an idea of the types of things offered:

1. Did you know that, if you have been a good-paying customer, you can generally get your initial telephone deposit back in one year *with interest*—if you ask for it?
2. You don't have to pay the phone company to provide telephone wiring. You can buy a special kit and do it yourself or probably save money even hiring a local contractor to do it for you. It pays if you have several phones and are fairly handy with installation and repair of wire.
3. If the directory assistance operator gives you a wrong number or if the number you seek is unlisted, you can get credit for that call. If you have someone in your home who doesn't see well, many phone companies offer free directory assistance.
4. If your phone service is interrupted for more than 24 hours, you can get a credit on your bill.

And there's lots more in the phone book's preface—goodies like vastly differing costs for various types of services, hours that you place the call, and whether an operator has to help you. The FCC is on the phone company's hide all the time about disclosure, so you can get the scoop straight from your phone book.

One wise miser's move that the phone companies are *not* obligated to tell you about is the multitude of long distance services that you can sign up for—MCI, Sprint, Allnet, etc. I really mean *etc.*; it seems a new one throws its hat in the ring every day. In addition each is constantly changing its costs, calling area, and so forth. The features of each are enough to boggle the best of minds, but they're worth checking out. Because each customer's needs are different, no one service is best for everyone.

Before I tell you how to determine the right long distance service for you, let me fill you in on how not to. Do not sit back and just wait for a salesman from one of the services to call you. Unless prepared, there is very little defense against one of these aggressive boys. A gift of gab is a prerequisite for their taking the job and most of them can make any service sound like the top one. Here's how to find out which one you should buy:

Take a pad and pencil in hand and answer the following questions:

> What cities do I call most often?
> Do I call Europe, and if so, where?
> What hours do I make most of my calls; are off-peak hours convenient for me?
> Do I make a large volume of calls?
> Do I make all my calls from home or will I want to use the service while traveling?

Get the toll-free 800 numbers of the services that cover your area and, with the answers to the above in mind, go to work. Call each and ask first about price. Most services charge by distance. The prices for certain cities can vary vastly, however, so ask each about the rates for two minutes to wherever your favorite folk live. Find out if the service has a monthly fee or minimum dollar amount of calls that has to be met. If relevant, ask about calls made traveling, calls during off- or on-peak hours, calls to Europe, volume discounts and what services they have. Some of the larger ones—ask—have 24-hour operators to assist you. Several of them will give you credit for wrong numbers or bad connections immediately. Others make you wait for the bill.

The biggies own space-age satellites up in the sky and, of course, you're paying for a piece of that. The smaller guys

A Fair Shake from Ma Bell

who are cheaper simply lease WATS lines. They have very few services and the connections sometimes can sound like someone is cooking popcorn by the phone. But, if you don't mind hearing that as long as you can hear more change jingling in your pocket, check them out.

Back to your AT&T bill. Every month when it comes, you should scrutinize it for any phone calls logged at one minute. Why? There's a good chance that these are wrong numbers or numbers you re-dialed because of a bad connection. They could even be calls that you thought did not go through but the other party answered and heard no one, so you called again. One minute is the shortest time span that the phone company logs. Their computer coughs up even a 10-second wrong number as one minute. Very few long distance calls are shorter than this time span, so there's a good chance it's a mistake. Now here's the good news. The phone company seldom balks at giving credit for a one-minute call.

A lot of folks feel guilty if they dialed a number wrong and figure they should pay for their mistake. No. Call the phone company's credit bureau and get credit. Same thing if you have a bad connection. Just don't talk over a minute or they'll decree that if you were enjoying that wrong number or the bad connection that much, you pay for it.

Look at the list of long distance calls again—carefully. If you find any long distance charges you don't recognize, don't hesitate to request that they be investigated. Especially if there are several, there is a chance someone could be "tapping into your line." Ask the phone company to conduct a WIRE TEST, which they will usually do free of charge. If they come up with nothing, they will investigate the charges by calling that number and using the latest private investigators' techniques to find out who's the culprit.

Another possibility is that a sneak has discovered your credit card number and is using it. Beware of switchboard operators who stay on the line when you're making a call from a hotel. Flea-bag hotels are renowned for this. A good dollars-saving tip concerning hotels is: make most of your calls from the lobby pay-phone. You'll avoid disproportionate hotel surcharges and petty thievery at the switchboard.

A unique feature the phone company offers but does not advertise is what they call BILLED NUMBER SCREENING. If you don't want to receive collect calls or if you suspect someone is charging calls to your number, ask for billed number screening to be placed on your line to stop collect and third party calls. This way, when a collect call comes to your number, an operator will intercept and ask the calling party if they wish to bill the call another way. Billed number screening does not prevent you from charging calls to your number because you will be given a credit card with a code number.

Small businesses can benefit from another unadvertised service. If you have employees in the field calling in collect to get their messages or report on their adventures, you should have Ma Bell issue your company individual employee cards. A fringe benefit is that you can keep track of who's calling whom at your company's expense. You can even arrange it so your toilers can only call the home office. Ask the phone company for a CALL-ME CARD.

Most folks think conference calls are reserved for big businesses who have fancy equipment. They don't know that they can surprise Grandma by having all of her grandchildren on different phones at once to sing "Happy Birthday, Dear Grandma." The kids can be scattered all over the world and no special equipment is needed. You just call the operator and set a time for her to get everybody on the line. You pay the person-to-person rate for each youngster called for the length of the call. There is one limitation, however. If Grandma has more than 58 grandchildren, a few might have to be left out.

Of course you know the difference in cost between direct dial and operator assisted calls. It's self-explanatory. If you are having any trouble and need an operator to help you, be sure and tell her you're having "trouble" or "difficulty" and want "direct dial rates." In fact, any time an operator intercepts for any reason other than to ask your number, confirm that you're getting the direct dial rate.

If you're having difficulty calling Europe, after you've made sure you're getting the direct dial rate say you want to talk with the INWARD OPERATOR. That's the operator in the country that you're calling and the best one to get you connected. Keep a note pad by your phone and jot down names of operators who have helped you with any special problem. They are the ones who will testify for you if any perplexing charges show up on your bill.

I talked with a man who calls himself a "communications consultant." This resourceful chap makes a not-so-small fortune by merely analyzing people's phone bills. He charges *no* fees for his service because he is so confident he will find that the phone company has been charging you too much. His sole profit—and it is a whopping one—is taking a percentage of the money he saves you. It's a good gamble because he says he finds mistakes on 80 percent of the phone bills he analyzes. He told me that over the years there have been millions of dollars in overcharges! And, since he takes 60 percent of what he saves you, you can see why he makes a pretty good living catching the inadvertent thieves at the phone company. However, you don't need to call him and say, "Hey, would you like to take 60 percent of my phone savings?" He reluctantly divulged the very simple secret of his success—he *communicates* with the phone company. He looks at your phone bill and then *asks* them what they're charging for. You can do this very simply once you learn how.

What are some of the most common ways of overcharging? Ma Bell's (and all of her clones) favorite blooper is billing you for equipment and services you don't have—call waiting, call forwarding, three-way calling, a fancier phone, a non-published number—ad infinitum. These may have been things you originally ordered but never received, or things you had at one time and discontinued. Or, it just may be a phone company muck-up. Pay special attention to the bill following any change you have ordered; did they charge correctly, did they drop the charge of the discontinued item, etc. The hieroglyphics on your phone bill are becoming more and more complicated, so it's practically an impossibility to determine what you are paying for.

Do yourself a favor. Call the phone company and have them analyze your equipment and services and explain to you exactly what you're paying for. Ask for an EQUIPMENT INVENTORY FORM. You can even tell them that you will only pay for your bill when this itemization is finished. If you find that you have been overpaying, get a retroactive refund. There is no statute of limitations on this. The phone company is pretty good about giving you the refunds you deserve. Your phone check-up should be done annually.

Another of Ms. Bell's pranks is charging you each time you place an order with them. The defense is to always get the "order number" when you make a request. If you have to call back to add or delete something from the order, give that number. This way they will not decree it a new request and you can probably avoid the extra charges.

If you have any trouble with your service representative, do not hesitate to climb the corporate ladder of your local phone company. The phone companies have well-defined heirarchies with very strict rules. (Some people would call them "up-tight.") It took me over 10 calls to get the following information. When asked about the pecking order, three operators took my number and said they'd call back—they didn't. Six gave me their supervisors, who were also evasive. Two just hung up. And one brave operator finally coughed up the story. Ex-operators have told me that "it's quite a professional caste system at phone companies. Operators can be wiretapped by their superiors." However, you can usually get things resolved if you know how to climb high enough. Here's the story:

If your SERVICE REP or OPERATOR can't help you, ask for the SUPERVISOR. Everybody knows that. But it doesn't stop there. If the supervisor can't help you, ask for the MANAGER (day or night shift). Still no satisfaction, you ask for the DISTRICT MANAGER. Want to carry it further? Go to DIVISION or REGIONAL MANAGER. They're all so "conscientious" (aware of their personnel records) that you'll get help somewhere up this road. I've known the PRESIDENT of the local phone company to be awakened at home to help a customer with a problem.

Tip: Use the letter of commendation to good advantage here. If you get good service from a local representative, write that person's supervisor a congratulatory letter. The rep will never forget you, and the next time you want charges dismissed or otherwise need help, you've got a friend at the phone company.

I now want to introduce you to the magic of the "corporate collect call." There are scores of different types of businesses who will accept collect calls from their customers. I cannot give assurances here that any particular business will in fact accept your call. However, countless numbers of banks, travel agents, telephone companies, stores, investment firms, utilities and other companies have accepted my collect call as a matter of course. You needn't feel plucky about this. It's done all the time. You call collect for the company from "a good client" or "potential customer" and, if you get turned down, no harm done. Merely re-place your call direct.

Another big money saver is the toll-free 800 number. "Sure, I knew that," you say. But you, too, would be awestruck if you saw the mammoth listing of all the companies which have 800 numbers. There are two 800 number directories—Business and Consumer. The business book has about 200 pages of wholesalers, manufacturers and other numbers of interest to businesses. (There are lots of savings for you by buying direct from manufacturers and wholesalers; see the chapter on making miscellaneous major purchases.) The Consumer book has a surprising listing of free calls. Both publications cost under $10. Before you go placing expensive calls to airlines, national store chains or big companies in the next town, dial 1-800-555-1212 and let the operator's fingers do the walking and penny-saving for you. That call is free too.

If you're considering an answering service for yourself or your business, do a little detective work and determine which services in your city cater to the performing professions. Usually there are actors and actresses working there and they sound much better than the usual service's mealy-mouthed rejects from the phone company who put you on hold while you contemplate their nasality.

Buying something in response to a telephone sales call? Don't. Not unless you see a brochure or other legitimizing literature with addresses and guarantees on it. Never give to charities over the phone without same. Their brochures should disclose how much of your contribution goes to the charity, and how much to the organizers. Telephone solicitation of inferior or non-existent goods is a big racket. Steer clear. If you don't want anyone trying to sell you anything on the phone, submit your name to the "Direct Marketing Association" in New York City. They will remove your name from any national telephone solicitation lists. Only problem here is that you may receive *no* national solicitation calls. Even if you've asked Montgomery Ward to call you as soon as those new thingums to fit your widget come in, you may miss that call if your name is on their no-no list.

The secret of saving money on your phone is simple—ask about everything. Ma Bell's army has a big fat book which they call, appropriately enough, "The Bible." This magnum opus is brimming with special free features, special costly features, their complicated pricing structure... even how they have to be polite to you. So don't be afraid to ask. Nobody will snap at you or penalize you. You're the customer (all the more valuable to AT&T since poor old Ma Bell has been dismembered)—and compliance is part of the phone company's strict curriculum.

Getting Rock Bottom Prices for Radio Advertising

Are you one of the two hundred million people in this country who stands in awe of anything considered THE MEDIA? The average American spends several of his waking hours every day mesmerized by the tube, and television advertising has the uncanny power to make a *product* a household word almost overnight.

One television commercial can also cause a small businessman to lose his household and become a pauper overnight!

More affordable—and sometimes even more effective—is the game of radio advertising. But, like any sport, you can win only if you learn how to play the game, and then plan and execute your moves well.

Sometimes the canniest folk at a radio station are not the ones whose personalities fill your living room, talking to you, introducing music, and informing you of the sports, time and weather. The real sharpies are the RADIO TIME SALESMEN. At most stations, they earn more than the "talent" (as the on-air personalities are called).

And these sales shrewdies know two things about their product: One, what they have to sell is thin air, and it is impossible to put a real dollar value on it. (That's to their benefit, because they can jack its value up to whatever you will believe.)

Two, they know that once it is not sold, that minute is lost forever. There are no rummage sales on time that has gone by. (That's to your benefit, because they want to sell you the time right now.)

Let's start at the beginning. You are a businessman and you are considering advertising your restaurant, your bookstore, your catering service, your barber shop, or whatever, on radio. Let's say you are a media neophyte and, like the rest of this country, are stupefied by the media and its costs.

Your first step is to turn on your own radio (or a radio in the vicinity of your store or service). Listen around the dial for which stations come in clearly. Write down their call letters. Then listen to the "personality" of the station. Is it a rock station that appeals to younger listeners, or is it what is called "easy listening" or "middle of the road," which would appeal to a slightly older set? Interview stations have a lot of retirees tuning in, and all-news stations are listened to by countless professionals and businessfolk. Then you should consider what group of people your product or service appeals to. Try to make a match, and write down the names of those stations.

Now, listen for an hour or so and count the number of commercials on that station. Most importantly, note if they are commercials for local retailers or services. Some products such as soft drinks and airlines are purchased by huge Madison Avenue advertising agencies. These "shops," as they affectionately refer to themselves, impress their clients by the colossal number of stations they buy, and often the buyers have no idea of the effectiveness of an ad placed on any particular station. The local retailer, however, knows almost exactly how effective his advertising has been and he's not going to re-buy if it's not paying off.

You probably have a hot lead if you hear a lot of local commericals, and not all national/regional or what is called "public service" spots. When a station advertises a lot of charities and other good volunteer projects, you can think, "Good for them—being so socially responsible." True, you should applaud them for their benevolence, but also be aware that it means they couldn't get paid advertisers to buy those spots!

With your notes in hand, place a call to the station or stations you have chosen. Ask for the sales department and then say something like, "Hello, I'm John Jones. I'm in the retail business. I'm thinking of advertising on your station. Since it's the first time I'll be on your station, I want a 'bulk spot schedule' (that's just a fancy way to say I want to buy a number of commercials), to run for a four-week period. And since it's my first time on, I want a special consideration. If it works for me, I'll spend the dollars to make it worth your while." And, naturally, if it works, you will.

Then you ask the salesman what the station's POLITICAL RATE is. That will tip him off that you know his bottom line, because that's what a station's political rate is—the lowest possible price that it is permissible to sell time for. It's the rate the politicians get at election time and a station *cannot* go below that price.

Fat chance you're going to get that price, however, unless you give on certain points which we'll get to in a moment. The published rate is on a "rate card" or "grid card." You can always ask for a copy of the rate card, but that's for top dollar and you should not pay that. You should pay somewhere between rate card and political rate, depending on the time your "spot" (commercial) is on. The hottest time is called "morning drive time" from 6–10 AM. Next is "afternoon drive time" —that's 4 to 7 PM. It's called "drive" time because that's when a lot of people are driving to work and listening to their radios. You can expect to pay more if you insist that your commercial run then.

When your salesman tries to sell you his price, your best negotiating technique is this: "Look, I'm willing to be moved around. I don't believe people listen to the radio only when they're driving to work. Give me my price and I'll take RUN OF STATION." That means that the station can decide where to put your spot—a big dollar-saver. It's perfect for the station because, if they are sold out, they can move you to a time that is unsold. And it's not bad for you because, if you let them know that you would like to check the AFFIDAVITS, they will take special care to give you some good hot drive time along with the midnight specials. Affidavits are the documentation of when your commercials ran. Every station is required to send them to you.

Madison Avenue, for all of its avant-gardeism, has one archaic prejudice, one that you as a radio advertiser can benefit from. In days gone by, the major radio advertisers were food products, and food stores were six-days-a-week, nine-to-five businesses. (Now, what town of any size doesn't have a colossal 24-hour supermarket?) Therefore a prejudice against weekend advertising developed and, thanks to good old supply and demand, the prices of weekend spots dropped. As a radio salesman with 25 years experience on a top New York radio station told me, "Beats the heck out of me! You can still get valuable cheap spots on weekends." Do it! There are a lot of weekend listeners driving to the beach, cleaning the house and reading the paper with their radios blaring.

Back to determining station viability for a moment. Be sure to ask your salesman—before you agree to buy—what percentage of the station's overall advertising is local rather than regional/national bulk buys. You'll get the savvy-customer-of-the-year award if you ask the salesman what types of businesses are the bulk of his advertising, and how many of the local ones are repeat business. If you really don't want to gamble, you can even ask for the names of a few "satisfied customers." Call them. Tell them you are considering advertising on that station and ask, "How well has it worked for you?"

O.K., Foxy, you're already way ahead of the game. Now would you like to save an additional 15 percent on top of the great price you've been able to negotiate? See if this one flies: Tell the salesman that you want to put the account through your own agency. If you are a fairly big business, you might call your public relations or customer service person an "in house" agency. Any agency purchasing the radio time for you usually gets 15 percent of the buy. This is not a "kickback," it's a standard "commission." If you're a vest-pocket-size business with no "in house" capability, you can have your Aunt Hattie buy the time. Then the billing, affidavits, etc., goes to "Aunt Hattie Associates" (she does not have to be incorporated). And Aunt Hattie gets 15 percent of the buy. You work out your deal with Auntie.

Great, you've now bought a "spot schedule" at a good price and you're all set to go. But what are you going to say about your product/service, and who is going to say it? Several ways to go here:

1.) You can hire someone to write your commercial.
2.) You can write your own commercial.
3.) You can hire someone to perform and record your commercial.
4.) You can perform and record your own commercial.
5.) You can give the written spot to the DJ to perform.
6.) You can give a "fact sheet" to the DJ to extrapolate.

Make your decision on how comfortable you feel with writing or performing. It's usually the same price to have the DJ or host read the commercial as it is to give the station a tape of your spot. Remember, if you are writing the commercial, it has to be able to be delivered in *exactly* one minute (or whatever the length of time of the spot you purchased is). If you're a ham and have always wanted to hear the sound of your voice on radio—try it! The station ought to give you a little "studio time" and an engineer so you can record your own commercial. It might be fun. You could become the local Colonel Sanders or Frank Perdue (the old chicken boys). Your gravelly voice could captivate the community and, within a matter of weeks, housewives could be mobbing you in the shopping center, asking for your autograph!

That's not for you? Then the cheapest and most effective way to get a good commercial is to have the DJ or host/hostess of the show do it for you. Let the pro do the talking! You can either give the station a written commercial that the "talent" will read, or a FACT SHEET. This is one page of information about your product or service. The host has this in front of him, and he raps about the product/service from the sheet, and gives the phone number or address. (Be aware that at some stations there can be a talent charge if he has to write it from a fact sheet.)

You'll get a considerably better commercial if the DJ or host knows about your business first-hand. Best bet—invite the host out to your business; if it's a restaurant, give him and his wife a free dinner. Or send some of your product to him and then invite him to visit your store. That creates a personal relationship for the broadcaster with your product and, unless he's been taken to the emergency ward after eating in your restaurant, or mangled himself with your warped merchandise, his raves will have a ring of authenticity about them.

Last tip: Keep track of when the commercials ran by reading the affidavits you are sent. Make sure you get a MAKE GOOD if a spot was missed. Be sure you're happy with what the DJ is saying about your business. If you can't listen, ask the station for a tape of the commercial. Basically, just stay on 'em like a possum on a June bug, and you'll get your money's worth.

Saving Dollars on Travel

People who like to travel usually like people. People in the travel business usually like to travel. Therefore, people in the travel business usually like people—which means they like you. And what all this means is there's a whole lot of benefits and information on savings you can get just for the asking.

Unlike so many industries where you have to scrounge and fight to get your rights, a good travel agent or airline customer service representative is usually happy to get you the best deal possible—if you ask for it! Let me play my favorite refrain again, "To get the best deal, you have to be knowledgeable." You have to know your rights and what travel goodies there are. Then these amiable people-lovers in the travel business will give them to you rather than to those customers who weren't savvy enough to ask.

I can't emphasize enough the importance of a good travel agent who is interested in you and your business. For a frequent traveler, a good travel agent can be almost as important as a good gastroenterologist or podiatrist. Find one big enough to have the capability to find you the best deals, and small enough to give you personalized service. When shopping for a travel agent, ask how long the firm's been in business. You don't want some Johnny-come-lately who figures if he hangs out a travel agent's shingle, he'll get some free trips. Make sure that the agency has an Automated Reservation System. This is crucial. It's a big computer that has all airline schedule and fare information—and even covers hotels and car rental agencies. American Airlines' SABRE, United's APOLLO and TWA's PARS are three of the biggest. Lastly, it would be nice if the agency had a staff that had been round the world and could tell you first-hand about some destinations you are interested in. (With the unbelievable amount of freebies travel agents get, they all should have been!) Just for fun, let me tell you that travel agents are deluged with freebies from cruise ships and hotels. They get huge discounts on air travel and car rentals. They need just be on the International Association of Travel Agents list and flash their travel agent's card to become instant deities.

Now, if they didn't have to sit behind a desk booking reservations for you all year long so they had the time to take advantage of all these free rides, they'd be in really great shape. They'd also be a lot richer if they didn't have to make ends meet on their 10 percent commission they get from airlines, hotels, etc. Their small profit margin is one reason why travel agents usually can't give individuals breaks on their costs. If you travel extensively—I mean really extensively—or if you book quite a few tickets for a number of people, then your agent does have a little room to play. Ask what he can do for you.

Let's start with airline travel. Everyone bemoans all the confusion in air fares since deregulation. It is bewildering, but I will give you the general breakdown of fares at this writing. Also, with a little excavation work on your and your agent's part, you can unearth some pretty surprising savings. For instance, in many cases, when you're traveling from one city to another, it can be cheaper to buy two tickets—one to an intermediate destination and one to the final stop. Sometimes, depending on the special fares being offered, it's less expensive to buy a ticket to a further destination than you wish to go and get off at the changeover point (which is where you wanted to go in the first place!) This is often true when there are less expensive fares between the two coasts, which can be cheaper than the tab to Chicago in the middle.

The reason for having a good travel agent is that often these surprises don't show up on his computer screen, so a little detective work is called for. The computer system the travel agency has installed affects which flights are going to show up first in response to your request. If they have APOLLO, United flights will get first viewing. If they have SABRE, American's will, and so forth. A normally lazy travel agent will simply book from the first screens. It's up to you to nudge him into punching a few more keys so you get the very best fare. The head of the Travel Agents Computer Society said, "Answering the question of what flight is the cheapest depends primarily on how much time the agent is willing to spend to make the sale."

Also, if your agent has a lot of pull with the airlines and if a seat is available for full fare, the airline will usually accommodate the preferred agent and give the seat at the discount rate. But he has to ask for it, meaning you have to ask him to ask for it!

What I'm leading up to here is, in order to get this special care, either spend your whole life flying and buy through one agent *or* "schmoose" (that means be real nice) to a good travel agent. The rewards are manifold!

To help clear up some of the confusion and so that you can communicate more effectively with your travel agent, let's do a short crash course in airline fares.

The best deals are called PROMOTIONAL FARES. These are what the airlines call "capacity controlled fares." To us that means that a certain number of seats on a plane will be sold real cheap. Under this fare structure, two happy passengers could be settling down side by side for a pleasant flight—until Mr. Loser finds out Mr. Winner has paid only half of what he shelled out for the identical flight. If you have a basic understanding of airline fares, you can be Mr. and Mrs. Winner for all but emergency or last-minute business travel.

The next time you want to revive your Florida tan, call your travel agent as soon as you begin contemplating the trip. Don't just say, "What's the fare to..." Ask him, "What's the best *promotional* fare to Miami."

Here are the fare structures. They've been in effect for some time now, but, if they change, ask your agent for an overview and all will be revealed. I'm dealing with coach only. First-class high-rollers can skip the following frugal fare.

UNRESTRICTED COACH—This ticket is totally unrestricted. You can travel any day of the week, make any changes you like and buy your ticket just before departure. You pay through the proboscis for this.

APEX—This stands for "Advance Purchase Excursion" and applies to international flights only. You must purchase your ticket from 21-30 days before departure and usually have a 7 days minimum–180 days maximum stay in the destination country. If you make any changes or cancel within the 21-30 day period, you pay a penalty. Apex is about half the unrestricted coach fare. Everybody's happy. The airline has your money to play with for three extra weeks, and the country has a possible spendthrift loose on its terrain.

SUPER SAVER—This is the domestic version of Apex fares. If you can depart in midweek, there are extra savings. Also known as EXCURSION.

IT PACKAGE—This is a great low fare you can get if you are booking and paying for both airline and hotel (what travel agents call "land arrangements") ahead of time. Your agent merely punches into the computer that you are also booking and paying for a hotel, so you get the lower fare.

GIT FARES— "Group International Travel"—good only for groups of 10 or more. You can get them through your travel agent and there are great savings for folks who have the clan instinct.

CHARTER—Some real super savings here on non-scheduled airlines. Also some super hassles. If you don't mind your Monday flight leaving on Wednesday, or paying incredible penalties if you cancel, you might consider getting a charter through a travel agent or wholesaler. If you do, however, tell your agent that you're making out your check to the escrow bank account, which you'll probably find in the tour operator's brochure. On the front of the check put details of the flight. On the back, put "For deposit only." This can protect you against cancellation of the trip. If you opt for a charter (or if you are in ill health or fear that you may otherwise not be able to fulfill your prepaid vacation plans), Trip Cancellation Insurance is available.

Watch out for super-cut-rate tickets offered through newspaper ads or on your grocery store bulletin board. Chances are they are stolen and you're left at the airline counter detained, embarrassed and, worst of all, ticketless.

One sure-fire way to beat air fare increases is to take advantage of FARE PROTECTION. This is a consumer good-deal which allows you to buy your ticket far in advance of your trip. If the fare goes up, you travel at the cheaper price. If it goes down, you get a refund and can re-purchase. It's like "Heads you win, tails they lose."

It pays to have a good travel agent who will not only book the best flight for you, but one who has a bit of pull with the airlines. All flights are overbooked. If they weren't, the airlines couldn't afford to keep the planes in the air. So, often when you call an airline, you'll be told that the flight is sold out. Don't despair. Have yourself "wait listed" if it's still available. Then turn to your travel agent. Chances are he has some good buddies at the airline who might be able to do something for you.

Barring that, if you have to be on that flight, get to the airport very early. You'll be first on the stand-by list and it's a very rare flight when at least one stand-by doesn't get on. Whether you're on stand-by or not, get to the airport on time. Sure, you say, that's standard advice. But there are some special reasons for this. If the plane is too full, and you are "bumped," a lot of airlines will not only fly you to your destination on the next available flight, but also will give you a free round-trip ticket anywhere on their domestic system. But this maintains only if you have checked in on time. They are not required to do all this, but ask, and, chances are, ye shall receive. At the very least you will be given some money called "denied boarding compensation." Often, a Customer Service Rep will walk up and down the aisles of an overbooked flight and ask who would like to be given $50 (or whatever is being offered) for giving up their seat. Volunteers are then given the money and get to their destination on the next available flight.

If you are going to miss a meal by the airline's making you wait for the next flight, be sure and ask for a "meal chit" —a ticket for a free meal in the airport. If your wait is overnight, the airline will probably put you up in a hotel and let you wine and dine on their tab. Just ask.

There are lots of other peace offerings that many airlines will give you to keep you happy and flying with them. The possibilities of niceties are almost as varied as the imaginations of the Customer Service Representatives at the airports. I've heard of CSR's taking a family home for a week when they missed a once-a-week flight. They've mailed packages on their off-time for me. Once, when I was traveling to meet a cruise ship and my bags weren't on the flight, I was given $150 to buy some clothes to get me through the first couple days of the cruise until my bags could catch up with me.

Things like this are not covered by regulations, but, if you're upset, find a CSR, let him know your predicament, and you'll find some happy surprises.

One of the most effective ways of encouraging the representative to give you whatever perks he's permitted is to say something like, "I would really appreciate your doing that for me. In fact, I'd like to write you a letter of commendation. Who is your supervisor?" Presto! Watch his eyes light up with generosity. And then, of course, it's up to you to write a letter telling the boss what a great CSR you found. In most airlines (and other businesses) those letters are very important to one's career. And you can use complimentary letters as a very effective tool "in gratitude for favors you are negotiating to receive."

If your bag does not come through (and you've checked in on time), it is the airline's responsibility to get it to you—wherever you are—at their expense. If your bag is damaged, they must fix it for you—at their expense. If your bag is lost, the liability is very low and limited to personal effects. So let your valuables travel with you in the cabin.

If a delayed bag is going to put a big wrinkle in your trip, avoid checking bags through when there is a plane-transfer. Baggage transfers count for about 40 percent of misplaced bags. If you have the time between connecting flights, claim your bag at the transfer point and re-check it in to your destination. I've found that putting big, bright painted stars, ugly decals, plaid ribbons and other such eyesores on my suitcases helps immensely when claiming my bags—and is probably a big deterrent to baggage thieves. It's amazing to listen to the cacophony of "Is that our bag, dear? It certainly looks like it" at every airport baggage claim.

What, you got on the wrong plane? By law, the airline has to give you a free "futile flight refund" and then get you to where you wanted to go in the first place.

Before we go from airlines to ships and hotels, let me tell you that a few extra moments on the phone when you are making your reservation can make your trip a lot pleasanter. (Of course, you've dialed the airline's 800 number to save yourself the phone charges.) Request your seat numbers to avoid waiting in check-in lines. In fact, request anything you want—window, aisle, not over wing. On a 747, you might want seats in rows 11 through 18—smoothest ride and best visibility. Tall passengers might want the first row of a section just in back of exits for extra leg room.

Hungry? Ask for a seat near the galley (not right across from it—that's too noisy). Passengers close to the galley are served first. This is so pax (as the stewardesses abbreviate "passengers") don't die of starvation watching and smelling the trays pass by them to other passengers. If you're tired of airline dinner fare, get a vegetarian, seafood, even Muslim or Kosher meal. You don't have to be Jewish...

Many times I've taken a "special" bottle of wine on board and asked the flight attendants if my party can drink from that. It is usually permitted as long as the stewardess serves it to you. If you enjoy wine with your dinner, it can save on your booze tab and the stewardesses are usually very receptive to having happy passengers if they are discreet.

Ask your reservations agent about special car-rental rates offered to the airline's passengers. Ask about courtesy buses to your hotel. Ask about whatever you'd like and see what happens.

Thinking of a sea cruise? It's a great way to get around and avoid the hassles of trains, planes, and hotel reservations. A cruise is especially therapeutic for workaholics who are addicted to telephones. A ship to shore call is five dollars a minute with a three-minute minimum which is a good reason to go cold turkey on phone calls.

Groups of ten or more people can get a substantial discount or "one free per ten." Check with your travel agent—or better yet, the cruise line. Some travel agents like to take the "one free" from the "per ten" for their own use. Individuals and smaller groups can receive tremendous savings if they are not locked into a specific travel date. Ask for "space available" reservations. If a ship is not filled, there are great discounts to people who agree to go at the last minute. There's also a decent chance that you might be "bumped up" into a luxury cabin if you remembered to ask your travel agent to request TBA (to be assigned) accommodations.

Be sure to check out the cruise you're taking for more than just itinerary and length of cruise. All ships have different personalities—from quiet elegance to bawdy party. And you want to travel with compatible people.

The cruise lines' personalities can change throughout the years but, at this writing, my *subjective* opinion follows. Most of the cruise lines have several ships and there can be a great variance between them, so this is a very general view. Check with your travel agent and get specifics before choosing any particular cruise.

The following is not a rating of the cruises' itineraries, food, service, decor, etc. It is merely an indication of the type of passenger who tends to sail on them. For instance, Sitmar gives an excellent cruise. Their ships are lively and filled with throngs of satisfied passengers. They are graded "Buick" merely because people who sail on Sitmar are not usually the aristocracy seeking quiet elegance. They seem to be the fun-loving polyester set. And Used VW category here is no put-down. I've seen some great old push 'em in the pool parties and raucous beer drinking contests on Carnival.

ROLLS ROYCE DRIVERS TAKE: Lindblad Explorer or Sea Goddess Cruises.

CADILLAC DRIVERS TAKE: Royal Viking, Ocean Cruise Lines, Cunard's *QE 2*, Cunard/NAL's *Sagafjord* and *Vistafjord*, Holland American, Norwegian Caribbean's *Norway*, or P&O Princess's *Royal Princess*.

BUICK DRIVERS TAKE: American Hawaii, Paquet, Royal Caribbean Cruise Lines, Home Lines, Premier, Sitmar, and the other ships not mentioned above of P&O Princess, Cunard and Norwegian Caribbean.

CHEVY DRIVERS TAKE: Bahama Cruise Lines, Commodore, Costa, Scandinavian World, and Sun Lines.

USED VW DRIVERS TAKE: Carnival, Chandris, Eastern and Western Cruise Lines.

Keep in mind that older passengers tend to take the longer cruises, younger passengers take the shorter (especially weekend) cruises. Don't be overly influenced by the popular TV show, "Loveboat." With the exception of the crew and cruise staff (all of whom—it seems to me—are chasing each other around the deck all the time), I've seen relatively few on-board romances blossom between single passengers. Pack your own sweetie with your bags—and ships are great.

A cruise can also be a smart budget vacation if you keep your bar tab, gambling and in-port shopping to a minimum. If you like your spirits, take your own bar. The stewards will provide ice and pretzels free of charge, and cabin parties are perfectly acceptable. Take film and other drugstore items with you to avoid tremendous ship's store markups. Be watchful of the tours sold by the cruise line. Very often you can purchase the exact same tour directly from the operator in the port for substantially less. Figure tipping at the end of the cruise to be about 5 to 7½ percent of your fare.

When you're traveling abroad, pack your Diners Club and Carte Blanche in your wallet; leave your MasterCard in your carry-on bag. Let me explain. Credit card companies can get their currency from banks at the wholesale rate. This is tantamount to a discount at the shops and restaurants in the foreign country. The wholesale rate that they convert currency at is 3 to 5 percent better than individuals pay. Diners and Carte Blanche pass the full benefits along to you. American Express and Visa split it with you. MasterCard keeps it all! But don't depend on everyplace taking your Diners Club and Carte Blanche. Last time I was in Europe, Visa was the hot ticket. Each card's popularity varies around the world, so pack 'em all.

Unless it's contrary to the currency regulations of the country visited, I usually pack a bundle of one dollar bills. They're often taken in return for goods worth more than the currency conversion and it's nice to see the bell boy's face light up when he's given a greenback tip. It seems that George Washington's picture is beloved around the world.

By the way, if you are flying from one U.S. city to another to catch an overseas flight, show an agent the foreign ticket and save the 8 percent federal tax on the airfare. And don't buy travel insurance at the airport. It's cheaper from your agent.

One of the biggest missed savings is the corporate discount on hotels. Mr. and Mrs. on vacation often pay full price when, if Mr. told the hotel he worked for IBM or some other big corporation, he could get up to 20 percent off. ASK! Ask about what discounts they have. Also ask about weekend rates. Many business-oriented hotels have substantially reduced weekend and holiday rates. Check on seasonal specials.

When making your reservation (800 number, right?) ask for a confirmation number. This goes for your travel agent as well. Overbooking is spreading from airlines to hotels. Your agent's voucher lacks confirmation from the hotel and is therefore meaningless once you're on the other side of the ocean and your agent is home and sound asleep. Last resort, if the hotel says there is no room—MAKE NOISE. Amazing how rooms seem to be constructed while you wait in order to keep the noise level in the lobby down.

Always ask what their least expensive category is. Room rates often vary drastically within the same hotel. And the same room can cost a single much less than a couple. Some unscrupulous folk have been known to have one check in, and then both stay there.

There is one pretty sure-fire way to protect yourself against the almost customary extra charges on your hotel tab. For every service, tip in odd amounts so that the total ends in the same number, say 7. Then, when checking your tab, every room-service, restaurant or bar tab that doesn't end in 7 probably isn't yours.

A big rip-off is telephone sur-charges. Check the hotel's policy on this when you check in. A call from an overseas hotel to the U.S. can be triple the amount of the actual call. Make good use of your credit cards or the pay phones in the lobby.

It almost goes without saying, but unless you're a masochist—a glutton for humiliation—be sure to have your credit card with you before checking into a hotel. If you don't they can make you pay in advance, be rude about room service unless you pay cash, and generally treat you as a convicted deadhead.

Before you leave on your trip, peruse the chapter on saving on telephone calls, and study the car rental chapter. Then pack your valuables and travelers checks in your carry-on bag and have a bon voyage.

Getting a Great Fur for a Great Price

Have you ever glanced into a furrier's window? If you look in while the furrier is trying to sell his wares, you will see ordinary women transform themselves in their imaginations into sleek and exotic animals as they pose before the mirror swaddled in their potential purchases. You need just look at the expressions on their faces and watch their posturing as they pet themselves to comprehend the power of—THE FUR COAT.

The woman who is buying a fur has obviously dismissed any humanitarian·hesitation concerning the animal before entering the fur salon, so now it's the furrier's job to overcome any of her financial fears and convince her that the fur is— whatever she dreams it to be. Is it a once-in-a-lifetime indulgence she deserves? Or should he present it as a very sensible investment for the practical woman? Does she seek a status symbol, or a long-lasting coat for warmth?

The only defense against a furrier's psychological persuasion is to learn a little about furs and the fur business. And *not* from the man who wants your money. O.K., let's figure out if, when, where and how you should buy a fur.

IF—The "if" decision is left to you. Yes, some furs are a very sensible investment. Others are nothing more than an egoistic indulgence. Furs vary greatly in beauty, price and durability. This chapter will attempt to let you know some of the qualities of the most popular furs and a bit about workmanship so that you can better make your decision.

The president of the largest fur outlet on the East Coast told me that he's bringing his son into the business and, after five years, the kid's still learning. So don't expect to close the book after this chapter and be an expert on furs. No two fur coats in the world are alike. Naturally. No two furs could possibly be made from the same parts of the same animal.

WHEN?—Best time to buy is May and August. In May, the furriers are testing out their patterns. You can pick up some pretty good bargains then. In August, however, you'll get the best selection. In August, they're getting into the full swing of it and the larger furriers will have many coats to choose from. They have reason to give you a good price then, too. They want to see what's going to move so they can make more of those for the holiday season. Conventional wisdom says, "Buy at the end of winter." Sure, the prices do go down around the end of February and the beginning of March, but then you're getting only what didn't move that season.

WHERE?—Do not buy your coat in a department store. (Nix that tip if the fur department of your local store is run by an experienced and reputable furrier. But that's unlikely because what's a nice experienced and reputable furrier doing working in a place like that? If he's that good, chances are he'd be out on his own.)

The reason for not buying in a department store is that usually it is impossible to find out the history of the fur. It's a rare saleslady who has any idea of where the skins come from. Most of the salesgirls I have encountered know the price, what their commission is, and that's it. It's imperative to ask around and find a reputable furrier, preferably one who has been in the business for a long time and is a member of what is called the Master Furriers Guild. Membership in a trade organization like this is important, so you have someone to complain to if there's any problem. The furrier should be large enough to purchase skins and make his own coats, and small enough to take the time to deal with you and answer all your questions.

Another good bet if you can make a trip to New York is go to Fur Heaven—around 30th Street and 7th Avenue—where most of America's fur manufacturers and wholesalers are all piled on top of one another. They say "Wholesale" or "To the Trade" only. But don't you believe it. They like your money just fine. You can save about 30 percent in these shops—and probably another 10 percent if you speak Greek or Yiddish!

HOW—This is the biggie. First let's consider whether you want to buy your coat off the rack or have it made? A furrier who sells off the rack will tell you the former and a furrier who makes the coats will tell you the latter. Makes sense.

The price for either is essentially the same and there are advantages to both. When you have your coat made, you can choose and inspect the skins and have precisely the design of coat you want. If it doesn't fit quite right, the furrier will most probably work on it until it is right—up to a point. You should look very carefully at the skins, however, to make sure those are the ones that eventually wind up on your back. The old switcharoo number is far from unheard of in the fur industry.

Before you decide to have your coat made, be sure you trust your design sense. Lots of times a woman has chosen a design from a magazine and she visualizes herself looking just like Christie Brinkley flying across the snow barefoot and nude except for her chinchilla. When she dons the coat in front of her furrier's mirror, she's far from a fur fantasy and therefore doomed to disappointment.

Buying off the rack, at least you'll know exactly what you're getting. The only problem is that you have to choose from what the furrier has in the shop. You can still inspect the skins, however, by having the furrier open up the lining. The reverse side of the leather should be soft, supple and have a healthful feeling. The fewer seams, the better. Check the workmanship—the seams should all be lined up evenly. Look for the little markings on the back of the hide and ask where the skins are from. It doesn't matter beans that you don't know the difference between a Canadian or South African skin, because, in case you haven't guessed it, that question is simply part of the bargaining process. If you ask these smart shoppers' questions, your furrier will be more inclined to reward your supposed discrimination by showing you his best quality and giving you a better price. After all, if you know enough to ask where the skins came from, you must know a lot about price.

Then, turn the coat back over and check the length of hair all over the coat. Unless it's part of the design, it should all be the same. The way the pros inspect a coat is to splay it out on the floor and check that all of the seams are straight and that any lines running through the fur are evenly spaced. Do that and your furrier will scurry down to his vault to bring you a better coat.

Another test of a good quality coat is to run your hand against the fur. Compare it to the feel of your hair at different times. Sometimes it's been dried out from the sun. At other times, when you run your hand through your locks, they feel conditioned and healthy. That's how your fur should feel. Your hand should not even be able to get down to the leather. The fur should be so thick that you should not be able to feel the skin underneath. Ask him if the skins were dyed. Dying fur has become a very expensive process, so it is not so common in America now. Some furriers contend that dying does not injure the fur, but common sense would equate the effect of dying the fur of an animal with the effect of dying your own hair.

Your best bargaining power with the furrier is to be and sound knowledgeable. Ask him where the skins are from and where they were DRESSED. Dressing is preparation of the skins so they become supple and don't deteriorate. The hide is cured by putting it into huge vats where it is soaked to kill the bacteria. Finally, oil is put back in the skin and the hair is cleaned off.

For once, American workmanship wins. The word is that if you buy dressed skins from Canada or the Orient, some bacteria can be left inside which eventually deteriorates the leather. Therefore, try to get American dressed skins. Be wary of coats from Korea, Taiwan and China. All over the world, there are auctions of skins. And right now the lowest quality skins are going to these destinations because there're a lot of ready, willing but not-so-able working hands over there. They either make BLANKETS or full coats and sell them back to America. A "blanket" or "plate" is a large piece of fur, usually 48 inches long by 40 inches wide, sewn together from dozens of small hide pieces.

There is a town in Greece called "Kastoria." Every home in Kastoria has boxes of fur pieces from all over the world piled around the house. The whole family pitches in whenever there is a new shipment. First step is to separate the little skins into similar piles—same fur, same color, same length of hair. There is at least one sewing machine in each house and practically every man, woman and child spends most of his waking hours sewing pieces of skins together into these "blankets." These are then sold around the world to be made into coats. A coat made from these blankets is less expensive, but does not hold up as well.

If your budget permits, tell your furrier you do not want a PIECE COAT, which is one made from these blankets. Tell him you want a FULL SKIN, LET OUT coat. This means that the coat is made from the full skin of the animal and there will be fewer seams, and thus it is more durable.

Let's get on to kinds of fur. You'll want to consider beauty, durability and cost. Beauty is a subjective judgment. Durability is not. And cost can be whatever your furrier is charging and you are willing to pay!

What follows is an impossible task—a listing of the most popular furs in descending order of price. The reason I say "Impossible!" is because a multitude of factors affect price—the vast range in quality of fur, the workmanship, where the skins were prepared, the design and fashion of the coat, the season it's purchased, and, of course, who's selling it. The only way to get this information from furriers was to demand it from them at verbal gunpoint. What follows is a very general listing, in descending order of price, and includes my furriers' caustic comments.

LYNX

"One of the most beautiful furs in the world. Doesn't wear worth a damn. Glamorous, sexy, dynamic fur—too damned expensive. I've sold three in 35 years. One was to Zsa Zsa Gabor—couldn't talk her out of it. She paid $55,000 for a lynx jacket." DURABILITY—3.

SABLE

"Cream of the crop. Rare and lovely. Very light to wear and I'd give it an A+ in warmth. Very durable but not quite as good as mink because it's got a little longer hair and you gotta be careful it doesn't break off. Who was it, Taylor. Yeah, I think it was Neiman Marcus sold Liz a $125,000 sable. Now your Canadian sable is nowhere near the quality of Russian." DURABILITY—8.

CHINCHILLA

"Lightest fur in the world. Beautiful. But the leather part is so tissue-thin that you raise your arm and it rips. It's very rare I'd make a long coat. Little coverups and jackets, maybe. Not that great a seller. It's an occasion piece." DURABILITY—2.

MINK

"O.K. here's your all time best fur—biggest seller, biggest price range, most adaptable to any fashion, and super warm. I check my minks when they come in for storage—they hold up well. Especially the male—has a heavier pelt and wears longer than the female. Female's silkier and slimmer and a bit lighter, but they're all good. Just like humans, the female's more expensive." DURABILITY—10.

FOX

"Now there's a big range in fox. It's a high-fashion fur and you gotta take a little care with it. Some are very lightweight but bulky. And it varies. Blue fox is stronger than your red because it's thicker and plusher. But your red is more expensive. Red fox is a wild animal, blue is raised like mink. Look for a silky, not woolly texture—an' don't give it a lot of beating. Sometimes you can get a shedding problem. DURABILITY (Red Fox)—4; DURABILITY (Blue Fox)—7.

COYOTE

"Most coyote coats look like dog—some are pretty, though. The best ones have a whitish color. Look for clarity in color and a dense fur. It's a wild animal—better-wearing and doesn't shed as much as fox, but parts can wear. They look great for a year or two and then start to get shabby-looking. Very sporty fur. We make a lot of parkas with hoods. Good for skiing." DURABILITY—7.

SEAL

"Lasts forever! Kind of heavy but worth it if you want a long-lasting coat. Not as plentiful as they once were. The documentary about the clubbing of the seals in 1970 really knocked seal out of the market. But you can get them. Now the eskimos are clubbing the seals because they're eating the fish." DURABILITY—10.

BEAVER

"Warmest coat in the world. Only thing is, it needs to be cleaned and glazed more often because it's a water animal and it tends toward clumping. Years ago, every girl who went to college got a beaver coat so when she went to football games she didn't freeze to death. It's pretty long-lasting but because it's a long coarse hair, some parts can wear." DURABILITY—9.

RACCOON

"This is the one fur coat men seem to think they can wear and still be a man. Excellent wearing—guys still have the ones their dads had in college. Nice pliable fur. Look for a more silvery, silky nap, not coarse." DURABILITY—9.

PERSIAN LAMB

"Beautiful flat fur, but nobody wears them here. Mostly chosen by senior citizens now. Very popular in Germany and France, but here, I guess everybody associates them with their grandmothers. Years ago, everybody waited for their children to get through school and then rewarded themselves with a persian lamb. Heavy darn things, though. A little lady could hardly get it up over her shoulders. You gotta watch them after 10-15 years, the pelts start drying out." DURABILITY—7.

MUSKRAT

"Muskrat looks best when it's dyed and it's getting too expensive to dye furs today in this country. Dyed muskrat used to be real glamorous. Your southern muskrat is flatter, northern is heavier." DURABILITY—9.

POSSUM

"I give this coat a good rating all across the board. Low priced, beautiful, long lasting. It's a great starter coat. It can take a girl right through college." DURABILITY—8.

RABBIT

"I won't touch it." This was the sentiment of several furriers on rabbit. Rabbit sheds and is not long lasting. It's also the only fur that won't keep you warm. If a rabbit had to stay out in the snow, he wouldn't make it. However, it is super-cheap. DURABILITY—Zip.

Whether you're strutting out of the store in a lynx or a possum, a mink or a muskrat, you should have a bill of sale in your hand that gives you the type of fur and the country of origin on it. The FTC also requires that furriers mark whether the fur is natural or dyed. That way, you have some recourse if it starts to shed and you find out that your fox was really rabbit incognito.

There is no other business I know of where the adage "You can get a great deal if you know someone in the business" is truer. The next time you meet a furrier at a party, treat that charming rotund little chap as if he were royalty. A little scouting work pays off. There are many furriers who will give huge discounts to members of certain groups. For instance, I talked with a furrier who gives very special prices to anyone connected with the Pittsburgh Ballet. Why? Because the word spreads and dozens of ballerinas go arabesquing into his store. You needn't even know what a "plié" is, however. The fact that you mention the ballet company (or whatever his favored group is) can get you the discount.

Cutting the High Cost of Dying (Funerals)

This is a tough subject, so we're going to toughen up and look at some stark realities about an industry fraught with rip-offs. After a house and car, a funeral is the largest expense for the average American. And when tragedy strikes, what kind of position is one in to make a wise decision? If you are in the vast majority, you are deeply bereaved at the loss of a loved one (or guilt-ridden if you're not). You are inexperienced in dealing with funeral arrangements and totally unknowledgeable about costs. You have done no comparison shopping and feel it would be tasteless to bargain. To top it off, you have to make an on-the-spot decision. You desperately want to do the right thing but you have no idea what the *right* thing is.

In this dazed state, who are you looking to for guidance? The worst possible choice — a Funeral Director, an alert businessman who is thoroughly trained in graveside manner and crafty sales techniques.

You wouldn't dream of buying a car or house under this gun. It would be analogous to your family estate's burning to the ground and your turning to the nearest real estate broker for help. He sits you down, consoles you for a moment and then has you start to fill out forms while he confuses you with his version of legalities. You have never purchased a house before and have no idea of costs or quality. Your sense of good taste and your worry and grief prevent you from asking too many questions or bargaining. He then tells you your options—but only those which he wants to disclose. And then you sign on the bottom line because you have to move in tomorrow!

If you permit this situation to happen, *your* epitaph should read SUCKER. A fine, proper and meaningful funeral can be arranged for a departed one if you use some of your good sense *now*—before you are emotionally incapable and bound by ridiculous time constraints.

Before we present alternatives, let us go on a brief journey. I will tell you what usually happens when the funeral director takes your hand and guides you down his floral path.

When death occurs, you call the funeral home and they pick up the body ("transfer it," as the funeral director will say), and then you come in to meet with him. After a few minutes of mellifluous professional consolation, he brings out some forms for you to fill out. This is for the death certificate, or "vital statistics form." Of most interest to him, of course, is "occupation of deceased," which can be a fairly good indication of wealth, and "death benefits," which, to him, translates into how much money you are able to give him. Your funeral director probably knows to the penny the death benefit payments of all trade and governmental organizations. In hushed tones, he says that he will take care of getting death certificates for your insurance and other legal purposes.

He then begins to ask you certain questions. Unless the funeral director is rare and unusually principled, he will probably start routinely requesting your choices, such as, "What hours would you like for viewing? What time would you like the ceremony? Shall we provide the funeral sedan and flower car in addition to the hearse ["casket coach" he says to us.] May we assist you with the cemetery or flowers?"

Right here is where you should, in your mind, shout a loud "WHOA!" This is the beginning of his very subtle sales pitch for the *traditional ground burial*—the most expensive kind. He will not tell you this, but you have several beautiful and dignified alternatives to this expensive send-off which we will get into shortly.

He's banking that you, in your stunned state, will just continue answering his questions, which will lead you into the full services of the funeral home. Fortunately the Federal Trade Commission now requires that written prices be submitted to the customers ("family"). Some states are enlightened enough to require a breakdown of specific costs. Prices vary throughout the country, but a usual markup on optional funeral items is 200 percent.

To give you an idea of general costs, I've included a typical price list in the Appendix that by law must be placed in front of the bereaved during the sales pitch. Notice the n/a (not available) in front of a less expensive item, such as the unfinished wood box, and prices like $3.75 per acknowledgment card. Where else does a little *card* cost $3.75? Look how much more expensive it is to forward remains to another funeral home rather than bringing it in—and those costs don't even include shipping. Then there's $75 for a make-up job, $150 for an hour of viewing, and $300 for a service in *your* home. All of the above don't even include the fee for funeral director and staff!

The funeral director creates the image that he is minister and guide to help you understand the American tradition of burial. This kind "grief therapist" gently helps you with your decisions at this difficult time. This is not to say that all funeral directors are ghoulish swindlers. Some can be very instrumental in helping one though the bereavement process—I've met a few in my research. But they are constrained by the competitiveness of the business and the wide acceptance of the disporportionate markups. At their conventions (which, by the way, are as raucous and convivial as those of any other group of salesmen), they are trained in techniques designed to get you to buy their most expensive services.

One of your first choices will probably not be presented as a choice at all: whether or not to embalm. Funeral directors often will hint that embalming (replacing blood with other fluids) is required by law. Practically all of them, if asked, will tell you that it is a health measure to prevent the spread of disease. On the contrary, there is no law or religious doctrine whatsoever that I have encountered that requires embalming, and there are no health hazards to the living by not embalming. In fact, except in North America, embalming is rarely performed. Many cultures find it gruesome.

Since funeral directors are required to ask you whether you want embalming or not, many choose a sneaky way around this by asking their question, "What hours would you like for *viewing?*" The fact that you choose "viewing" will be taken as an affirmative on embalming. Sneaky, huh? Indeed, if you do choose an "open casket ceremony," embalming is aesthetically recommended. But, again, open casket ceremonies are popular only in North America. The rest of the world is appalled by this concept, which has been perpetuated by the National Association of Funeral Directors. The NAFD teaches its members to play heavily upon the concept of everlasting "memory picture." "Seeing the loved one peaceful and comfortable in his final resting place helps one through the grief process" is the basic theory they are promulgating.

There is a high profit in embalming—a lot of dollars for a few chemicals. The funeral director charges another fee for make-up, and this opens up the discussion of burial clothing—you may even be offered women's lingerie for the departed, or "stylish and comfortable" shoes which don't even show! "But naturally, you will want the best for your dearly departed."

You can be assured that a trip to the casket room will be on your agenda. In this room, caskets are artfully lit and arranged taking into account studies of psychology of buying and natural human traffic patterns (when left alone, most people move in a circle to the right)—all aiming you toward the most expensive caskets. Often a funeral home is "temporarily out" of a certain inexpensive model and obviously you are in no position to wait for "the next shipment." Thanks to the hype of the funeral industry, long gone is the *real* American tradition of family and friends and carrying the dead in a plain pine box to the grave.

Once you have chosen the casket and think your underground funeral expense is over, you will be hit with one of the latest ploys for making money—the vault. "What?" you ask. This is an outer casing to "protect" the coffin. You will probably be told that, without a vault, "the coffin could disintegrate and the land might cave in" or even that it is a law! Don't you believe it. There is no law concerning vaults, although some cemeteries that receive a percentage of the vault sales will only accept coffins in vaults.

The rip-offs don't end with the funeral home. You can pay double the first-class train fare for shipment of the dead and double the air-freight charge for plane travel. The cost of cemetery plots is astronomically higher than the cost of the land. Newspaper notices, florists, even ministers manage to get themselves into the profit side of death. And it goes on and on.

There have been several instances where one book has changed the course of human events—*Unsafe at Any Speed* by Ralph Nader, *Silent Spring* by Rachael Carson, *Uncle Tom's Cabin* by Harriet Beecher Stowe. There is another: *The American Way of Death* by Jessica Mitford. The book is crammed with the chicanery of the burial business. It is the definitive work on funeral rip-offs and should be read by anyone who might be faced with the death of a loved one.

Rather than continue in this vein, however, let us get right to the bottom line on how to orchestrate fine and respectful last honors for a departed one, and still have some money left over to be enjoyed by the living.

The single most important counsel I can give is *Do Not Wait Until Death Occurs.* Plan the final rites now when you can make rational decisions, and perhaps even consult with the aging or ill family member. The FTC also requires that prices be given by funeral homes. You may call around and get quotes on prices. Tell the funeral directors you are doing some PRE-NEED RESEARCH. When you use their insider's term, "pre-need," he'll know you're up on the industry and you can be sure that you will get better prices and arrangements—a whole lot better now than when you are emotionally unable to bargain and they hold all the aces. If you plan ahead, you can order an appropriate coffin and find a cemetery which does not require a vault. You can pre-plan a home service with your clergyman—not one overseen by the funeral home.

Most people do not realize that they can have any type of farewell they choose. And with each of the following, you can create any type of service you deem appropriate. Here are some of your alternatives in descending order of cost.

1. The top is, of course, the TRADITIONAL GROUND BURIAL with embalming, open casket, viewing hours and all the et-ceteras mentioned above. This is the funeral director's fantasy.

2. The next is IMMEDIATE GROUND BURIAL. This is self-explanatory. It avoids the cost of embalming, viewing hours, and might even help a family avoid a "keeping-up-with-the-Joneses" style casket. Some families will accompany the coffin to the graveside and then have a service afterward. Keep in mind that a service in your home or at your club or place of worship can be equally if not more meaningful, and a great cost saver.

3. Next is CREMATION WITH MEMORIAL SERVICE AND VIEWING. Those who choose this or the following alternative should know that a beautifully fashioned or meaningful container provided by the family can be preferable to the standard one preferred by funeral directors. Be prepared for a little resistance and having to sign a "release," because they

would prefer to sell you their own $400-plus jar. One of their favorite tactics is to convince you by telling you they can't "guarantee the remains in your container."

4. IMMEDIATE CREMATION is the next choice. Perhaps the most beautiful last rites I ever experienced were those of a dear friend, an artist who had been killed in a plane crash. His family, though very wealthy, chose immediate cremation with no frills, and his ashes were scattered across his land. Six months later, after grief had subsided a bit, a "Celebration of His Life" was held. It became an almost joyful event attended by his great circle of friends. One artist let fly 100 white balloons into the sky. Others gave tribute in song and dance. John Lennon and Yoko Ono even performed a dramatic silent song to his memory. This was an innovative tribute to life and not a concentration on death.

5. Finally, there is DONATION OF BODY TO MEDICINE. There are many medical schools around the country who will accept the body and, when finished with their research, will cremate at their expense and return the remains to the family.

Fortunately there are organizations in our country dedicated specifically to helping people make difficult funeral decisions. They are called Funeral or Memorial Societies and can be found through telephone information or by contacting the Continental Association of Funeral and Memorial Societies in Washington, D.C. To date, there are over 150 of these societies and, for a small membership fee, they will present you with a whole panoply of options. They also have arrangements with certain funeral homes that will offer their services at a reduced cost.

Even without joining a memorial society, you may be able to obtain these "discounts" if you treat the purchase of a funeral like any other product or service and bargain rationally ahead of time. Your funeral director thinks of it as a business—why shouldn't you?

What I am saying is, quite simply, consider your choices *now*. Think ahead so that you are not forced into expensive options that you may regret later, not only because of cost, but also because you feel that either you, your family or the deceased might have wished otherwise.

Life in a Plastic Society, or How to Clear Up Your Credit Rating

There is one way in which we definitely deserve being called a "plastic society"—IN OUR DEPENDENCE ON CREDIT CARDS.

Today, if you don't have a major credit card, you are seen as a possible car thief to the car rental agent, a midnight-skip to the hotel reservations clerk, and a no-account to a business associate when you plunk down cash at a business lunch.

Try a day of travel without your plastic passport. Car rental agents can ask for up to $300 cash deposit. Hotels ask not only for cash up front, but a deposit to cover any extra charges you might incur. You often can't even make one phone call from your room if you haven't laid out the green at the desk to cover it when you checked in. And at lunch, watch your associate's face when you pull out a wad of bills. He's thinking "What's happening? Is my genial host trying to evade the IRS? Is he laundering money? Worst of all, can't he *get* a credit card?"

A good credit rating has become almost a necessity to deal effectively in today's society. Without a good credit rating, you don't get the necessary plastic. And, without the plastic, as the comedian Rodney Dangerfield would say, "You don't get no respect!"

How do you get a good credit rating? I was naive enough to think that all you had to do was pay your bills on time. That definitely helps, but it's not the whole story, especially when applying for your first credit cards. You get a good credit rating by being lucky enough to fall into the "right category" in a complicated statistical analysis of people just like you.

Let's start at the beginning. You apply for your first credit card—a Sears charge account. (This is one of the easiest to get.) You fill out an application asking you for some personal data like your birthday, number of dependents, etc. You scribble down some things about your home—whether you own or rent, how long you've lived there. Then there's some employment information and, of course, *"How much money do you make?"* After you tell Sears about your bank accounts and other assets, you sign a little microscopic clause at the bottom of the form which says that you are authorizing Sears to "investigate your credit-worthiness."

You figure that if you make enough money and have a pretty good repayment record on other accounts, you're a shoo-in. Not necessarily! Your chances are better than average that you'll get the card because, after all, they're in the business of extending credit. But there is one wrinkle that the average consumer doesn't know about.

You could be the victim of what is called THE SCORING SYSTEM—a complicated contrivance called "discriminate analysis." All your answers are thrown into a giant computer and are compared to those of other folks who were good payers, bad payers or non-payers.

Sears sends your data into a CONSUMER REPORTING AGENCY, more commonly known as a Credit Bureau. The Credit Bureau, for a fee from Sears, punches up all the information they have received on you from various credit grantors—charge accounts, banks, other stores, etc. The Credit Bureau's computer then compares your information with people in their files who have given similar information—and they arrive at your score. This is the computer's "opinion" of how good a payer you will be.

The computer stacks you up against information gathered over the most recent three-year period. For example, if people who lived at their current residence between two and four years were good payers in the past three years and you have lived in your home for three years, you're in luck on that particular calculation. If people who have four children were lousy payers and you have four kids, you get a black mark in that category. And so on and so on until they arrive at your fate.

They then give your score to Sears and it's then up to Sears to decided whether they want to take a chance on you.

Here's some good news. If they decide not to extend credit to you, you have the right (also in the small print at the bottom of the application) to ask them "why?" They are obligated to come up with a reason. But they don't just say, "Because you had a sleazy score." Sears goes back to the Credit Bureau and asks which categories you failed in. Then the store chooses one to tell you. Chances are they are not going to say, "It's because you have four children." Although that could be the cause if, in the past three years, people in your area with four kids had a poor repayment record. A better choice for Sears would be to tell you something else on your record, like you were slow in making your payments to your local department store.

Even if they respond with this, however, all is not lost. Armed with this bit of information, you can now attempt to clear up your credit rating. As an individual, you are permitted to review your own rating. Sears is also obligated to tell you which Credit Reporting Agency gave them the incriminating evidence. There are, by the way, five major

Credit Bureaus in this country. You simply call them and tell them you want access to your record. You can go to their headquarters there and review it or, for a nominal charge, they will send it to you. If you go, you'll need two pieces of identification. Naturally you cannot review anybody else's rating—only yours.

If you feel something is incorrect in your report, you are permitted to contest it. It's called, understandably, a "dispute." It's important to know that, often, rather than spend the time and money to check it out, they drop it. Even if they do verify the blacklisting item, you are permitted a one-hundred word explanation to be entered into the record.

Say that you feel your bad department store repayment was because you thought you were paid up and were out of the country for two months. Fine, enter it. It's then up to Sears to decide whether to believe you or not. And all subsequent credit grantors will receive your explanation with the printout.

The whole thing is something of a Catch-22. Even though you've given them pause on your payment record, you still have four dependents. And you're not about to clear that up!

Credit Seeker, take consolation in one fact. It's a lot better than it used to be. Before credit bureaus, computers and the scoring system, you were out of luck if you were one of the "Four P's" or "Three B's." The Four P's were painters, preachers, plumbers, and prostitutes. The Three B's were barbers, beauticians and bartenders.

Don't ask me why the above professions were a poor credit risk. But then don't ask me why people who lived at their residences between two and four years are better risks than others. It's just plain old-fashioned subjective probability scoring versus "sophisticated" computer probability scoring.

Can you cheat? Not really. You don't know what the good guys and the bad guys filled out in your area in the past three years.

Life in a Plastic Society 133

Now there are certain things that the Credit Bureaus *cannot* use against you—race, creed, color, national origin, sex, age. The Federal Government says that if you are over 62, you must be judged the same as the next lower age category. However, age falls into the scoring system too.

Seems pretty arbitrary, doesn't it? Well, it is and it isn't. Statistics are meaningful, but only as meaningful as the interpreter of those figures. And at least now you know you have a way to fight back if you don't agree with the interpretation.

Eating in Fine Restaurants—For Cheap

Dining out these days is an expensive form of nourishment—and entertainment. It is the restaurant's obligation to give you your money's worth, not only in food, but in service, respect, and creating a thoroughly enjoyable experience for you. Unfortunately, even many of the finest restaurants lose sight of this fact. They become jaded and give their best only to those customers who somehow prove to the restaurateurs (self-ordained judges of status) that they deserve it.

Restaurants are one of the institutions where the *price* of the food is not negotiable—even for their "regulars." But by incorporating a few little tricks presented in the first part of this chapter into your repertoire, you can sail through the dining adventure getting the best food and service, and be treated with all the deference accorded the restaurant's most favored patrons. The second part will concentrate on getting you out of the restaurant free of the most common form of restaurant malady—indigestion caused by looking at the steep tab.

Starting with your phone reservation, the maitre d' makes a judgment about you which is going to affect how he treats your party when you enter his turf. How you look and conduct yourself when you enter is going to affect how long you wait for a table and which table you get.

But let's go back to the beginning. You're calling to reserve a table for four people on Saturday night and you're not sure they can accommodate you. Don't just call up and say, "Could I make a reservation for tomorrow?" Come on strong. Know the maitre d's name. (Find it out by phone a few hours earlier!) Say, "Hello Max, this is Mr. Martin. We'll be a party of four tomorrow night at eight. Please save us a *good* table." Then it's up to Max to go through a guilt trip because he can't remember who this dynamic Mr. Martin is. When you arrive at the restaurant, remind Max that you are Mr. Martin. Reinforce his memory with a few dollars. Oil of palm is very popular in fine restaurants.

There are certain tips which I am hesitant to give. Not because they don't work—they do! But because certain tricks take a pluck and brazenness that only the most audacious readers will feel comfortable following. Here's one: When you call Max for your reservation, say this is *Doctor* Martin. (Restaurants accord doctors Most Favored Status because they usually earn/spend more). If you're going to pull off this ploy, however, just hope that there are no heart attacks, chokings or unexpected births in the restaurant Saturday night or that may be your Last Supper there.

Other reservation tips: The best time to call is the day before (immediately preceding or just after the peak meal hours). If you call too early or late, the maitre d' will be on his break and probably will not be answering the phone, so your reservation might get lost. Conversely if you call at peak service hour, he could be so busy that he forgets to put down your reservation. Call about three in the afternoon, and, if you're not pulling the Max ploy above, get the name of the person taking your reservation. This way, if there's any problem, you and the maitre d' will know who is at fault. There are too many Saturday night sneaks at popular restaurants who try to convince the maitre d' that they had a reservation but "It must have gotten lost." That one seldom flies, so, armed with the name of your reservation taker, Max will know who's corrupt and who's credible.

One final reminder on reservations: There is usually no need to confirm but, if you're taking an important client out to dinner and you want to make sure there are no screw-ups, you might call earlier that day and say, "Max, I'm bringing Mr. Stuart to dinner tonight so try to make sure we have our table on time." Doesn't matter who Mr. Stuart is, but if the tone of your voice makes him sound like he's the Dali Lama, you will be treated accordingly.

By the way, it does pay to get to know the maitre d' well; ask about his family, his children—make him feel like a person and he'll feel more at ease being your humble servant. In addition to the appropriate tipping, an occasional gift will emblazon you in his memory so you can get one of the best tables on *any* Saturday night.

Getting a good table: Best advice is ask for it! Note above when Mr. Martin called he said, "Save us a *good* table." Then, upon entering the restaurant, remind Max, "I'm Mr. Martin. You said you would save us a good table. Is it ready?" It will be.

If there is a certain table you want, get to know the restaurant. When you are dining there, ask the number(s) of the table(s) you like. Then, when making your reservation the next time, ask that a certain numbered table be reserved for you and, unless Frank Sinatra has called earlier for that table, you'll get it.

How you look when you enter the restaurant is going to win or lose you a lot of points with respect to your deferential treatment. The best way for a man to score high is to cross the threshold with a beautiful well-dressed woman on his arm. Conversely, a woman finds a good-looking fashionable man the best weapon for getting top treatment in a restaurant. This is sometimes hard to arrange, however, so come to the establishment looking well-heeled yourself. Maitre d's like to "dress the room." They arrange the patrons attractively with as much care as they place the tables or arrange the flowers.

It sometimes helps to know the owner's name and, when

you enter, casually ask if he's there tonight. If he is, he'll probably drop by your table later. Introduce yourself and tell him how much you appreciate his establishment. If he isn't there, you've made points with the maitre d' which will count toward your getting better treatment.

On to saving money! As I have said, the prices are firm but you can save a lot by ordering well. Know the prices of food in grocery stores and order the dishes with the least markup. For instance, if a restaurant charges $16 for a steak, they've paid $9 for it. This is the same dining room that charges $12 for a pasta dish, and they've paid only a dollar for the ingredients. Omelettes are another penny saver's folly. For fifteen cents worth of egg and onion, you might pay six dollars. A restaurant can never charge enough for caviar compared to what it pays for it, so they make it up on soups, casseroles and other concoctions.

Another high mark-up item is coffee. You pay a dollar for a dime's worth of this refreshment. Have your coffee relaxing at home afterwards and save.

Have your cocktails at home or at a less expensive establishment. One of the reasons that tables are often "not ready" when you arrive is that they want you to spend time at the bar. The greedy restaurateurs put you in the cocktail lounge, ply you with thirst-producing peanuts, and watch your tab mount up. Why not enjoy your cocktails at home and, as you're getting ready to leave, call the restaurant and ask if your table will be ready when you arrive? The call helps assure that it will be.

Dieters and penny pinchers alike will enjoy the "one entrée stratagem." Often I've gone to the finest restaurants with a friend (after substantial hors d'oeuvres at home) and said to the waiter, "We're not hungry tonight so we're having just one cuisses de grenouilles sautees between us, but don't worry, that will not affect your tip." Sounds crass but it isn't. Waiters and captains are percentage people. The largest part of their income is from tips, so they are very aware of how much you're ordering. After the meal, tip as though you'd ordered two main dishes and your one-entrée party of two will be welcome anytime.

If you do get a surly waiter, call him on it. Putting up with an impertinent server can ruin an otherwise fine evening. Say something like, "Georgio, is something bothering you today? Did I insult you?" I've never failed to see a reversal in attitude once it's brought to their attention.

Do *not* let the restaurant get away with spieling off a list of specials without giving prices. When your server comes to you and asks if you'd like to hear today's specials, respond with "Yes, very much, and the prices please." Too many restaurants play on the patron's desire to appear unconcerned with price—and then they sock it to him on the check.

To get the finest fare the kitchen offers, it's good to know the head chef's name. Ask the waiter at the beginning of the meal, "Is Mr. Cabrini on tonight?" If he is, you might want to add that it would be nice if he could oversee your meal. You can be sure your comments will be passed on to the kitchen and extra care will be taken. If you frequent a restaurant, a complimentary note on the back of your business card to be delivered to the chef is a good way to assure that he will take extra care the next time he hears you are in the restaurant. One note, head chefs are usually off Sunday or Monday night. In Chinese restaurants, it's almost a law that they don't come in on Mondays. Plan to eat home on Sundays and Mondays.

A quick note for fish aficianados: Never order fish on Sunday because no fresh fish is delivered on that day.

Tuesday through Thursday are the best evenings for dining out. You avoid the weekend rush, and can be better taken care of. Lunchtime offers great bargains. It's the same food, same preparation, same service, lower prices. Some of the finest restaurants offer the same fare at lunch for practically half the price.

A restaurant's markup on wine can range from a lot to ludicrous. If you have a special wine you would like to have with your meal, call the restaurant ahead of time. Tell the maitre d' that you would be very happy to pay their corkage fee, but that you will be bringing a very special wine that you would like to have with your meal. The corkage fee will range from one to twenty dollars. Twenty may seem very high, but if you are a connoisseur of fine wines, you will save considerable money. This is not something that should be repeated many times at the same restaurant, since a good part of their profit is from wine and liquor. A good standard money-saver is to frequent restaurants which do not have a liquor license. There is no corkage fee for bringing your own spirits to these places.

A restaurant is like a wine shop. Often they get specials, and when they run out of that particular wine, that's it. If you find one of these specials on your favorite restaurant's wine list, you may purchase a case from them and they will keep it in their wine cellar for you.

If you are one of the many people who get pleasure from being treated like a celebrity, there is one sure-fire way to achieve VIP status at your favorite restaurant. Go there regularly and take out a house account. This way the restaurant saves the credit card charges and it is passed on in the form of gratitude and good will toward you—and an occasional free cordial or no charge on your wine tab.

Bon appetit!

Hidden Treasure in the Trunk of Your Rental Car

When it comes to renting a car, forget every generalization you've ever heard about specific companies. Even *Consumer Reports*, which makes judgments on everything from Acne to Yogurt, doesn't touch car rental companies. It seems their prices change every day.

Each time you want to rent a car your price is a roll of the dice, and you could win or lose depending on:

1. The time of the year.
2. The day of the week.
3. Whether it's a holiday or not.
4. What business you're in.
5. Where in the country you're renting.
6. What airline you flew on.
7. What hotel you're staying at.
8. What specials or promotions they're running.
9. How knowledgeable the reservations agent is.

Most people either just call their favorite car rental company and make a reservation or have their travel agent do the honors. Don't be that lazy. You're missing out on a lot of discounts and goodies if you are.

Keep the 800 numbers of all the major car rental companies in your little black book and, before you rent a car, devote 20 minutes to the project of getting the best deal by calling each of them and asking for their least expensive rate on the dates and in the city you are going to rent in. You could save hundreds of dollars this way. In addition to the major rental companies, get the numbers of a few local ones from telephone information in the city you're traveling to. Call a few of these companies and compare their rates. This must be done each time you travel because their rates are constantly changing depending on various combinations of the factors above.

Some companies have unlimited mileage, with you paying for the gas; others charge by the mile; and then there are some that offer a choice between the two. Before you decide which to take, estimate your probable number of miles and calculate whether an unlimited mileage or a pay-by-the-mile deal is better. (Whichever you choose, ask where the least expensive gas station is and fill the tanks upon return. Even if you go to the most expensive neighborhood station, gas will be cheaper than the rate the rental company will charge you.)

Don't make your choice solely on the low rates, however. The reservations agents have hidden treasure in their computers that most of us never know about—but which you are about to be handed the key to discovering. Every week the major car rental companies run special promotions that are advertised only in certain publications as a trade offer or to encourage a segment of the buying public. You and I would normally never find out about them unless we read every magazine and newspaper in the country. The agents are not supposed to reveal them unless you make a specific request. It's one of those deals where, "If you tell me you know about it, I'll tell you *all* about it."

Here's the key. After the clerk has given you the prices on the cars, say something like, "I read about some special promotion, but I've forgotten specifically what it was. Isn't there some airline discount or other special promotion or giveaway you're running for this city?" That will probably get you the information. If not, ask for the "Promotions Department" and try again.

I called the major companies and told them I was traveling to Miami next week. Using the script above, these were the freebies I extracted.

HERTZ—If you rent a car for five days (not necessarily sequential) at the daily rate, you will get an Eastern Airlines ticket to any city on the East Coast for only $29.95.

AVIS—For the same five rental days, they offered a ticket to anywhere on American Airlines' or Republic's system for $49.90, or anywhere on NY Air or Air Cal's routes for $19.95. That means you could fly New York to Los Angeles for $49.90.

Here's an interesting bonanza. For even a one-day Avis rental, you could get a coupon for two free one-day cruise round trips from Miami to Freeport in the Bahamas on a luxury liner. All you had to do was pay the port tax and a small food charge—and know to ask for the coupon!

BUDGET—Their normal rates were $39/day, and $119/week for a compact, but if you were flying United Airlines and knew to ask, that same car would be $12/day and only $8 for a subcompact.

NATIONAL—This company was running a "Florida Drive-Out" special. They gave you a free car to drive to almost any city on the East Coast—if you asked for it.

And these were for just one city! The major auto rental firms have hundreds of similar promotions, but they are in a continual state of change. The above were in effect only at the time of this writing.

If you can't take advantage of any of the current promotions, your choice will probably be based on cost. Don't forget to ask about drop-off-charges and insurance costs. They could easily tip the scales. Many people forget they are entitled to discounts. Do you belong to AAA? Do you work for a big company? If so, chances are your company is registered with them and you are eligible for a corporate discount. Those of you in the travel business already know you can get up to a whopping 50 percent off.

Once you've gotten a price over the phone and a car you're happy with, be sure to get a reservation or confirmation number and the name of the clerk who informed you of it. If, when you get to the car rental counter, they say they don't have your $10/day Lincoln Continental special, you'll be on much stronger footing. They usually come up with the deal if you have a name and number.

Don't be misled by what they call the "weekend rate," thinking it's only Friday through Sunday. It's the kind of weekend most of us would love to have. The weekend rate is valid from Thursday noon to midnight Monday and can be a big bargain. Depending on the time of year, request an "off-season" rate. Often I have been promised off-season rates only to arrive at the counter and find the clerk knows nothing about it. That's where the reservation number comes in handy. You should know that if they don't have the car you reserved, they must give you a more expensive car at the same rate.

Pack your plastic. Car rental companies are extremely "credit card chauvinistic." Without a credit card, they usually ask for a deposit in the neighborhood of $300.

Some of the smaller companies have a lower daily rate but insist that you take their expensive daily insurance. They will hint that you have no coverage if you don't. This is incorrect. All rental cars must have insurance, and your own insurance probably covers you too. What the optional insurance does is to eliminate the collision deductible, which can be from one to five hundred dollars. Ask each company in advance what their deductible is and, all other factors being equal, go with the lower deductible. I usually bypass their insurance, drive extra carefully, and take a gamble on the deductible.

It's a tough question whether to go with "Number One" or "The-Company-That-Tries-Harder" if their rates are close to Number Three on down. I have found that the top companies usually come to the rescue quicker if there is a mechanical failure, and their cars are a little cleaner and better equipped.

A short checklist before leaving the counter: Make sure your rate is written in on the contract. Ask, "What is the grace period?" (the minutes or hours that the car can be returned late without being charged another day). Then get a map and you're on your way.

Before driving off in your chariot, check the car for little dents and scratches and ask the attendant to make a notation so you won't be charged for them later.

Be sure to allow enough time to return the car and get your receipt. Many a mathematical mistake has been made after your contract is in the drop-off box at the counter. Also there are hefty penalties for leaving the car in the airport anywhere except in their lot, which can be several miles from your departure gate. A $75 punishment showed up on my American Express bill last time I tried to get away with leaving it by the departure gate.

Winning at the Food Game

The average American householder spends over an hour a week in a semi-dazed state shuffling up and down the aisles of a supermarket grabbing product after product and building a big expensive clump in a basket. At the end of the trance, the score is tallied and it is usually an uncontested victory for the supermarket. Thanks to clever packaging and strategic placement of products, the consumer has purchased more than he or she needs. The ordinary shopper is as predictable as a mouse following a trail of cheese into the trap.

Motivational experts and their hired gang of merchandising mavens have advised supermarkets to make their carts larger. Have you noticed? They are about 30 percent larger than they were ten years ago. And it's because studies have shown that many weekly shoppers only head for the checkout when they can't jam one more chocolate Twinkie in their cart.

When people are excited and alert, they blink their eyes much faster. In a study, Vance Packard (the *Hidden Persuaders* man) showed that shoppers in the market hypnotically blink far slower than normal! The purpose of this chapter is, with a fingersnap, to pull the consumer out of the trance and open lazy eyes to the tremendous savings that the smart shopper can realize in the supermarket. You will also be introduced to some $-saving alternatives to shopping at the same commissary you've been frequenting for so long.

Before I go any further, let me state that the Supermarket Boys are not all bad. In fact, they work pretty hard in this extremely competitive, low markup field in order to convince you to return week after week for their wares. But even in the honest pursuit of profit they have to pull a few in-store maneuvers that you should be aware of.

First, let's case the layout. Nothing is left to chance. The Supermarket Psychologists have done their homework—they've studied shoppers' traffic patterns. High-profit items are placed right where you walk in when you still know you have some money jingling in your pocket to pay for it. Produce is high-profit impulse stuff and is often placed in aisle one. This is "Start" for your path through the maze that they predict you'll follow. Believe it or not, you can start your savings program by walking to the other end of the store and working your way back against the tide of shoppers pushing their carts clockwise around the store. This makes you less susceptable to the hidden persuaders' tactics.

There's another clever placement at the end of your journey—the checkout counter. It's all part of the grand scheme of things that they put candy, gum and other goodies right at the checkout where moms are trapped in line with their irritable and hungry kids. Same thing with magazines. Boredom makes you grab one, you get hooked on an article, and they've made a sale.

You can't hide from the marketing geniuses even in the middle of the aisle in the center of the store. Studies of shoppers' scanning habits have shown that items placed at eye level move much faster. Here's where they place more of the expensive impulse items. The staples—flour, salt, sugar, etc.—are usually placed on lower shelves so you have to look at everything before finding them. The most expensive products (or those with highest profit for the store) are placed about five feet, four inches off the floor.

Unless you are a mathematical whiz and can do complicated division in your subconscious, you should choose a supermarket that has "unit pricing." In addition to the price of the product, unit pricing gives the price per weight, volume or size so that competitors can easily be compared. This price-per-measure system is not a law—yet. But you should reward the stores that voluntarily choose unit pricing. And you'll be rewarding your pocketbook as well.

Be wary of what we'll call "Implication of Sale" items. These are twofold: One is the mountain of product at the end of an aisle with a big cardboard price tacked to it. The other is the "twofer" (or "threefer," "fourfer," even "fivefer"). Often these mountains and multiples are not sales at all but duds that the store is trying to push. Mid-aisle bins or casually placed shopping carts filled with tasty morsels also fall into this implication of sale category.

Any smart manager will place produce at one end of the store and the dairy section at the other so you will have to traverse the whole store to buy your lettuce, milk and eggs, thereby subjecting yourself to box after jar after can of brightly colored products shouting "Buy ME!" at you. Your only defense is to make a list of what you need before entering the tempting terrain.

And the subtle psychological persuasion goes on and on. Your only defense is to stay alert, look up and down (not just at eye level), know exactly what you want, where it is—and go for it. If you could blindfold your kids at the checkout, it would help, but...

Let's talk about WHEN to shop. In some stores you should avoid the beginning of the month. That's when welfare and social security checks come out and many a market has been known to raise its prices for a few days. Usually, Tuesday and Wednesday are pretty good days because the newspaper ads come out then and stock on sale items is pretty high. And the lines are shorter. To get the best selection and top freshness, the wise thing to do is to ask your store manager when meat, poultry, and produce are delivered. I've been in supermarkets on Monday mornings looking at case after empty meat case because their meat deliveries were Monday afternoon.

For both taste and frugality, it's best to buy fruits and vegetables in season. In the Appendix you will find a chart called "When It's Good and Cheap" which tells you what to buy, when, for maximum freshness and minimum cost. Fruits and vegetables at fruit stands? Not necessarily! I was shocked to discover that often the same produce distributor who delivers to the supermarket makes a delivery at your fruit stand. And often you pay for that "from the earth" feel of the outdoor produce mart.

I think I got the definitive word on WHERE to shop when one of the grocery store managers I was talking with said, "The grocer's biggest enemy is the car." That's right. Grocers know that the bigger the supermarket you travel to, the higher the savings for you. Non-inner-city stores have lower overhead and more space to hold on to non-perishable items. So they have a better selection and hopefully will pass some of the savings from their low overhead on to you. If they don't, pass on them.

Also use your car to get to the supermarket offering the best prices in any particular week. Check the midweek and Sunday papers. Then go to the store that advertises the best specials for your appetite and pocketbook. Buying large quantities of true sale items also is a big $-saver. You will find a chart in the Appendix which tells you what you can freeze and for how long.

The vast acres of food and products which has become known as the Supermarket is a great and growing American tradition. It has become so popular, in fact, that meager little corner stores have come to call themselves "superettes." "Super" to reflect supermarket, "ette" to denote smallness—a prefix and suffix only. Where's the "market"? These small stores are to be avoided for regular purchases, as are health food stores. It's my subjective opinion, but when I look past the bizarre concoctions in health food stores and the wrinkled and puny little vegetables touted as "organically grown," the only really healthy thing I see is their markups.

There are some good savings in STORE BRANDS and NO BRAND products. Research has shown that store brands with the store's name on them are usually as good as name brands and about 15 percent cheaper. If it's a non-namesake house brand (like A & P's "Ann Page"), it usually means they're not bragging about it and the quality may not be as high. It's a hung jury on those white boxes called "No Brand," "Generic" or "Money-Saving Brand" food. You can save about a third on cost, but for taste, you be the judge.

There is one tremendous source of savings in the supermarket that I am loathe to get into because I don't want to be a hypocrite. I must admit I have no patience for poring through newspapers and junk mail, scissors in hand. I don't relish the thought of little pieces of paper sticking out of counter drawers and collecting grease behind cookie jars. But millions of Americans can't be wrong; people save many millions of dollars by CLIPPING COUPONS. And for that reason, although not a practitioner, I am a total advocate of coupons and refunds.

You find them everywhere—in the stores, in magazines and newspapers, in home mailers, enclosed in the product packages; some clubs and libraries even have a box on the shelf of "give some–take some" coupons. There are many homemakers who trade their coupons. For instance, a family with a baby but no pets will trade coupons with the pet-no-baby family. Also called "cents-off" or "cash-off," these little paper scraps can save you hundreds of dollars a year on your grocery bills. Coupon aficionados swear that they can take up to 40 percent off their regular food bill through concentrated coupon clipping. In fact, if you really get hooked on this game, there is a monthly newsletter out of Yonkers, New York called "Refundle Bundle" (Box 141, Centuck Station, zip code

10710). It will keep you apprised of all the latest and sophisticated couponing techniques, including a coupon clearing house! If you have the scissors and the patience, read on.

To avoid kitchen disarray and to get the best use of your coupons, take a pile of envelopes and label them with categories of products you usually buy such as "Breads," "Paper Goods" or "Coffee." Then put your clipped coupons in these envelopes, put a rubber band around the package, and pack it in your purse the next time you go marketing.

To avoid impatient and grousing customers in line behind you at the checkout counter, put all items which will be purchased with coupons in one part of your basket. To avoid the fisheye from the checkout girl, tell her before she starts punching buttons that coupons go with a particular pile, and this way the process will be almost at full speed.

There is no need to feel "chintzy" about using coupons. The store management is thrilled you're using them because, in addition to the face value of the coupons, manufacturers give hefty handling fees to the stores for their trouble. Some stores are so enamored of your coupon use that they have "Doubling Days" when they credit you with double the face value of the coupon.

Refunds are the next big saver. Susan Samtur who wrote *Cashing In at the Checkout* (and also swears you can save up to 80 percent on what you buy through coupons) averages a whopping tax-free $1500 per year in refunds. However, I think that amount is minus her overhead in stamps, ball-point pens and scissor-sharpening! Refunds are the little bribes manufacturers send you for trying their products. Have you ever seen a check for 25 cents? Start refunding and you'll get one six to eight weeks later. They can add up.

Let's get on to quicker savings. No matter how magnificent your supermarket is, there are money-saving alternatives. You don't necessarily have to own a diner to buy your food wholesale. Look in your Yellow Pages under "Meat—Wholesale" or "Frozen Foods—Wholesale" or "Whatever-You-Are-Looking-For—*Wholesale*." Call them up, place a fairly large order, and go pick the goodies up. They're not apt to turn you down if you buy enough. You might want to get together with several families in your neighborhood and make one big purchase.

By doing this, you have the beginning of a BUYING CLUB. These proliferate around the country. To find one in my community, however, I had to call the Chamber of Commerce, which then turned up several. These are definitely worth checking out, especially if you are feeding a big family.

Quite a few big corporations have a FOOD BUYING COOPERATIVE which works the same way as the buying clubs. You place a weekly order along with other employees, and one employee is elected to pick the order up and it is distributed. Ask your personnel manager about it. If your company does not already participate, there might be sufficient interest to start one. A very large percentage of your food bill can be saved this way.

If you like beef and have a big freezer, you might consider buying a whole steer—or at least half, called a "side." A side is made up of a "hind quarter," which gives steaks, and a "fore quarter," which is ribs, chuck and stewing meats. A good wholesaler will usually cut up the meat to your specifications and wrap it for the freezer at no extra charge. The price per pound is substantially lower than the Supermarket's. Again, check your phone book—"Meats—Wholesale."

No matter whether you're buying wholesale or retail, with coupons, or without, there is one best defense against getting ripped off on food costs. It's a simple thing that many of us fail to do. It's this: Stay awake while shopping and make a mental note of how much each item costs. Most of us have a pretty good idea of how much a quart of milk or a loaf of bread should cost. But do we really know how much frozen asparagus tips should be?

Knowing the going rate on food is all-important. You can

see big bold red letters advertising a sale in Wednesday's paper on asparagus tips but, unless you know the usual price, how can you tell whether it's a real sale or if the grocer is pushing some leftover stock at full price? The size of the sign in the store is no indication either. Knowing the going rate on food will help you realize when a sale is really phenomenal so you can stock up. Coupons will begin to make sense to you also. Twenty-five cents off on an item that costs half a buck more than its competitors is no big deal. But you won't know that unless you've done your homework. And, by knowing how much things should cost, you'll find yourself automatically rejecting little delicatessens and other over-priced shops.

It's a safe bet that shopping for food is a pastime that you are going to be involved in for the rest of your life. You might as well get smart about it. That way it's a game that becomes fun—almost.

Rent-a-Bus at the Pro's Price

Renting a bus—or "chartering a coach," as those in the business would say—is one negotiation where you cannot escape being pitted against the pros. When the time comes that you face the (hopefully no more than once in a lifetime) task of bringing 40 people from the city out to your daughter's wedding at a country church, or a litter of kids to your son's bar mitzvah, you'd best be prepared with a little "bus-speak" or you'll pay top dollar.

Ninety percent of the buses chartered are by motor coach tour operators. Another five percent comes from miscellaneous sources, such as the taking of airline crews to hotels, rural factory workers to their job, or school kids on field trips. People chartering buses for these reasons are repeat users and will get a fairly good price. However, you, the one-time user, could be a one-time loser if you're not careful. So, let's change that and put you in the driver's seat.

First, a few don'ts. When you're calling the bus company, don't ever say, "I want to rent a bus." You are *chartering* it. Better yet, you are chartering a "coach." Don't blither beginner's questions like, "Is it safe? Is there air-conditioning? Do you have any buses for 60 people? Is there a bathroom? How can I be sure he'll show up on time?" You'll be branded as a neophyte and you'll pay for the time the bus operator uses to educate you.

Answers to the above are:

1. Don't worry about safety. All buses have to pass rigorous safety requirements and are inspected by the State Department of Transportation every six months.
2. All buses built in the past 20 years have both heat and air-conditioning. They may not work, but they've got 'em.
3. Every full-size motor coach has between 45 and 53 seats. Keep your party under 53—no bus in America holds more.
4. Nothing wrong with wondering about the loo—it's a real concern! Most have them, but the word "bathroom" exposes the green behind your ears. And forget "toilet," "blue room," "john," "powder room," "latrine," "washroom," "little boys room" or any other euphemisms that have stuck with you over the years. To the bus-folk, it's a LAV.
5. Not to worry—no need to pad your departure time. Ninety-nine percent of the time the driver will show up early. It's his job.

Start your journey with your fingers, walking through the Yellow Pages to "Buses—Charter & Rental." Then, before you pick up the phone, write down a few things. Decide where you want your group picked up. That's your ORIGIN. Your destination is called, quite simply, DESTINATION. If you have any stops, write them down in the geographic order of your itinerary.

The coach operator calculates his price on a combination of time and distance, so let your opening salvo be information on times and distances. You might say, "Origin is the corner of Main and Broadway. My origin time is 8:30. We'll load there and departure from origin is 9:00. First destination is XYZ Company where we'll LAYOVER over 1 hour. Final destination is the Holiday Inn, where we'll be spending three hours. Departure from destination is 3:00, returning to origin at 5:00." If you use the "in words" and get right to the bus operator's bottom line in this fashion, he'll assume you are a volume user, and your coach will be priced accordingly. Tell him his "IN-SERVICE time will be 8½ hours" and that will clinch it.

The time/distance/price formula includes only the time when you are using the bus. The distance to you from his garage is his concern. Don't let him charge you for DEADHEADING time. That's the time when the bus is empty and the driver is bringing it to you.

Your next question is, "What type of equipment do you have?" There's no need to go into detail here, but, basically, there are only four types of full-size buses. If he replies with names like "Prevost," "MCI-9" or "Eagle 10," you'll know he's giving you his top of the line. There is an analogy here to the McDonnell Douglas aircraft numbers. A DC-10 is a big shiny new bird. A DC-3 is an old crate, reliable but not too classy. The lower the number after the MCI or Eagle, the older and probably the more of a tub the coach is. For bargaining purposes, you should know about an old work horse of a GM bus which is still very functional. It's known as the DECK or DECK AND A HALF because you walk up several different levels. This bus is affectionately referred to by the real insiders as the BUFFALO. A good lob when you're negotiating could be, "Gee, the tariff is a bit high. We don't need luxury, got any old buffaloes around?"

Ten or fifteen years ago, none of this charade that you're a volume user would be necessary to get the price down. The State Department of Transportation and Interstate Commerce Commission were very strict on charter bus prices. Your elderly Aunt Nellie's bridge club paid the same tab as the biggest tour operators. No longer. Coach operators still have their price or TARIFF on file with these departments, so why has it changed? Because it's no longer policed. The bus company can charge substantially above or below their tariff without fear of being brought on the carpet. By the way, if you feel you've been given too high a quote, you can ask what their "published tariff" is.

Let's suppose you've skillfully executed these complicated negotiations and are satisfied with your price. Now let's go for some guarantees and free extras that will make your trip pleasanter. The driver assigned to you can affect the mood of the whole trip. You don't want a driver who is going to bark at your Aunt Nellie, "Look, lady, you can't get on the bus by yourself, the heck with it." You'll have a better chance of getting a compatible coachman if you say you want a TOUR MAN. A tour man is one who is used to what the industry calls OVER THE ROAD WORK, or taking a group on a longer tour. If you don't ask, you could get what they call a LINE MAN—a driver who is not necessarily trained or experienced in dealing with people. You pay the same for either.

All the inspections that charter buses undergo do not immunize them from flat tires and other mechanical failures. Sitting with 45 people on the side of the thruway waiting for the bus's tire to be fixed is not anyone's idea of an outing. It wouldn't be so bad if the repair took the same time as fixing your car's flat. It doesn't. Huge special equipment needs to be brought in to put the bus back on the road. So be sure to ask ahead of time what the bus company does if there is mechanical failure.

The puny little operations will let you waste away by the roadside while they bring another bus from *their* garage, no matter how far away that is. A responsible outfit will immediately charter the nearest bus and get your group on its way. If you break down and discover it's going to be a while, call the bus company. The better ones will wine and dine your group or otherwise try to make life comfortable during the wait. But ye need ask in order to receive.

In your initial conversation, ask about their cancellation

policy. If you cancel several weeks in advance, there probably won't be a cancellation fee. But cancel the morning of your trip, and you can expect to pay.

The procedure once you've agreed on various points is that they will ask for a deposit, you'll ask for a confirmation, and you're ready to travel. If you're concerned about their insurance, you can call the ICC's 800 number and check if the bus is licensed to go where you're planning for it to go. If it is, it's got adequate insurance.

Keep in mind that supply and demand plays a big part in your price. The same bus, same number of hours, same number of miles is vastly more expensive on Saturday, July 4, than on the first Tuesday in November.

If you're willing to gamble and have a strong stomach, there's one sure-fire way to save a bundle on chartering a bus. Wait until the last minute. The bus operator's major costs are his driver and the diesel fuel. He vastly prefers your eleventh hour business to his bus sitting in the yard. If you're planning a trip on a Tuesday, it could be a wise move to check with several charter companies a few weeks in advance and see how their buses are moving. If, on the Saturday before your event, there are several buses available, you're probably in good shape. Then you can call up Monday and be in a much stronger negotiating position. If you can do this without losing any sleep, you've got yourself a good deal.

Insuring Rock-Bottom Auto Insurance Rates

Talk about a sweet deal for a salesman! Here's something that practically everybody *has* to have. It's so great that the government even mandates it. No driver in his right mind would ever want to be one moment without it. And there's lots of repeat business—people buy it automatically every year. The salesman doesn't even have to ask them! He can just sit back and collect his commission each time the policy rolls over. Not bad!

In fact, it's so lucrative that the competition for selling auto insurance has become pretty fierce. Now that's good and bad for you. The good news is that great prices are to be found. The bad news is that the agents hold their cards pretty close to their chests and you're going to have to develop some detective skills to unearth these bargains.

Here's a crash course that can save you up to 100 percent on your next policy.

The usual scenario goes like this. The insurance shopper calls one or two agents and says he wants to get a price on auto insurance. He then leans back, phone in hand and subjects himself to the agent's long list of questions. By passively allowing the agent to take control of the conversation, the shopper has irreversibly branded himself the novice that he is.

The trick is to call a broker and give him, up front, the five or six salient points that he needs to know so that his computer can cough up the price. (Don't assume that the price is fossilized in Fortran or Cobol, however. Unbeknownst to most of us, the agent's assessment of you plays a heavy role. But we'll get into that a bit later.)

To quote my insurance agent, "When someone calls me and he tells me everything I want to know—bang! bang! bang!—in the right order, I know he's called half a dozen other agents. And when a potential customer does that, he's going to get my best shot if I want his business."

"Why would he not want my business?" you ask. If you're a 22-year-old hot-rodder who sounds like an accident looking for a place to happen, you're not going to be too popular with insurance agents. If one insures you and the inevitable accident happens, the agent is going to get his wrists slapped by the company he's talked into taking you on. Too many bloopers like that and the big insurance company isn't going to give your agent his little (or not so little) bounty for good behavior at the end of the year. Or worse, they might raise their prices for all his other customers. Nobody wants much of this ASSIGNED RISK business.

Here's how an independent insurance broker works. He is free to purchase a policy from practically any insurance company licensed to operate in your area. He likes to develop especially good relationships with four or five companies, because if he gives them enough business, they reward them with special favors and a year's-end bonus.

Unless you have done your telephone-pricing homework and have chosen a company which deals only through CAPTIVE AGENTS, I recommend dealing only with independent brokers because they have more options to offer you. If you call an agent who deals with only one insurance company, that's all you can buy. In the business he's called a "Captive Agent." And you'll become a "prisoner" of that one policy.

If you want to be an especially savvy shopper, here's a tip. Look in *Consumer Reports* or *Best's* guide and find out the names of the big insurance companies and then see which ones are available in your area. *Consumer Reports* rates the companies on time in processing a claim, courtesy, what's covered, and how "chintzy" they are over dollar amount of damages. Interestingly enough, the companies with the best service also seem to have the best prices.

It's worthwhile to formulate some preliminary thoughts about which companies you would like to be insured by. Then, when you call your agent, see if he is free to get you a policy with any carrier and ask him which ones he works with most often. Before you've told him word one about yourself, you're ahead of the pack in his estimation. And, as I've said, his high estimation can mean lower costs for you.

Now we come in with the clincher. You are going to beat him to the draw on what he needs to know. If you let him proceed as he would with the usual greenhorn, he will ask you certain questions that he will need to feed his computer. Most insurance software packages ask them in this order:

NAME?
ADDRESS?
PHONE?
   That's so he can call you back with your price.
RATING TERRITORY?
   Where you reside has a rating. If you live in a big traffic-congested urban center, you pay top dollar. Insurance carriers log territory by county or zip code. Obviously you won't know your rating territory, but tell the agent your county or zip in this initial salvo.
HOW MANY AUTOS?
   It's cheaper to put your second or third car on the same policy.
HOW MANY DRIVERS?
YEAR, MAKE AND MODEL NUMBER OF AUTOS?
NAMES, AGE, SEX, MARITAL STATUS AND NUMBER OF YEARS ALL DRIVERS HAVE BEEN LICENSED?

HAVE DRIVERS HAD DRIVER TRAINING OR A DEFENSIVE DRIVING COURSE?
WHAT IS THE EXPECTED AMOUNT OF DRIVING OF EACH CAR BY EACH DRIVER? Over 25 percent of car usage labels one as a "principal driver."
HISTORY OF ACCIDENTS AND VIOLATIONS OVER THE LAST 3 YEARS
WHAT KIND OF COVERAGE DO YOU CURRENTLY HAVE? This is so he can be competitive and offer you the same or more at a better price.

Your answers to these questions are the data input for the magic number of what you are going to pay for your policy. Included in this equation is the all-important CATEGORY you are going to be put in: PREFERRED, STANDARD or (unfortunately for you) sub-standard, which they choose to call NON-STANDARD. If you're a fairly conservative driver with a good record, you should definitely settle only for an agent who is going to give you preferred rate status.

The tactic is to get your act together concerning the questions above before you pick up the phone. Pack as many answers into your opening thrust as you can. For instance, you might say. "This is Mary Jones. I own a home at 322 Main Street in Anytown—that's Montgomery County, of course. I have two cars, a 1985 Chevy Caprice and a 1975 Volvo, Model 164. I'll be the only driver. I'm 37 years old, divorced with two small children, have been driving for 19 years and have no current accidents or violations on my record. I'll be using my cars mainly to drive 10 miles to work each day. I'm sure I qualify for preferred rates and I'd like to get some quotes from you on one hundred thousand, three hundred thousand, fifty thousand liability for both cars and comprehensive and collision on my Chevy."

WHAM-O! Right between the eyes. That agent knows he's got no fool on the line. She knows the score and he's going to give Mary his best possible price. (By the way, that "$100,000/$300,000/$50,000" is agents lingo meaning $100,000 liability for one injured person, $300,000 for all people in the accident and $50,000 for property damage. It's a good amount for most people to carry, and in order for the agent to come up with a price, you must give him a specific amount like this.)

In fact, Mary is a winner in his eyes in another way. See if you can guess why?

Hint 1: She owns her home. It was no accident that Mary said, "I own a home at..."

Hint 2: She has two small children. Of course, they're not drivers, so why do you suppose Mary told him about them?

Answer: Mary knew that, like any broker who sells various kinds of insurance, he's going to be reading between the lines. "Aha, she owns a house," he says to himself. "That means if I do a good job for her on her auto insurance, I might be able to get her to convert her homeowner's policy over to me next year. And two small children! That means I can work on getting life insurance business from her." And that, for insurance brokers, is the real bonanza. On auto insurance, they get approximately 15 percent of the premium per year. On life insurance, they make a whopping 55 percent commission in the first year. This is called SUPPORTING BUSINESS and all-purpose agents always have their ears cocked for hints of that possibility. Hint away—it can lower your premiums.

Now, don't stop with this one good price. Call three or four more agents and go through the same performance. You can even play them off of each other, asking X why Agent Y was able to give you a better price. Spend one hour on this and you can save up to 100 percent on your auto insurance premium. Not a bad hourly wage for a little telephone work.

There are a few little postscripts you should know. One is that your driving record "washes itself" every three to four years. Depending on the state, any accidents or violations fall off your record approximately every 39 months. Millions of drivers who are currently paying "standard" rates could be bumped up into the "preferred" category merely by requesting a copy of their driving record from the Department of Motor Vehicles and showing it to their agent or shopping anew for a policy. Double check your classification because it could knock a good 15-30 percent off your premium. With several thousand policies, most agents are too busy to check their clientele's records to see who deserves the upgrade. That's up to you. He won't be upset. He may lose a few dollars in commissions but he's proud to have you climb a category because it helps his reputation and clout with the insurance carrier.

By the way, never switch policies mid-stream. Let one run out before buying another because your "refund" that is promised is SHORT RATE. And forget about premium financing. The only interest an agent has in arranging this with the bank is the kickback he receives, and you pay an exorbitant interest rate.

I'm assuming, of course, that you've checked with your company or any membership organizations to which you belong to see if there are any discounts on group auto insurance plans. If you haven't, do it. Can be big bucks savings here.

Finally, ask your agent for the discounts. If you hold a certain type of job (they love teachers, hate bartenders; don't ask me why), belong to a car pool or have taken a driver education course, the price can be lower. When you get right down to signing on the bottom line, tell your agent any goodies about yourself that might help. A Defensive Driving course which costs about $30 and takes a couple of evenings can completely pay for itself in discounts the first year.

Also, if you have any relevant changes in your life, don't neglect to let your agent know. If your teenager goes off to college and won't be driving any more, be *sure* and notify him. They are very prejudiced against teenage drivers and, for that, you can pay up to three times as much for your insurance! If you have a teen driver, make sure he drives less than 25 percent of the time so he's not logged as a principal driver.

As you can see, your premium is not "writ in stone." It's writ in statistics and in the opinion of your broker. The first one can't change. The other is very malleable. As my agent "confessed" to me, he many times just trusts his instinct when assigning a category to a client. So, you may dress to look poor for your dentist to avoid a high tab, but put your best conservative well-heeled foot forward when meeting your insurance agent.

How to Throw a Catered Party and Not Let It Throw You

Dealing with a caterer can turn your party into an overpriced calamity if you don't know precisely what you're doing. Experienced hosts and hostesses tell their caterer exactly what they want quickly and efficiently. This permits the caterer to be caterer—not teacher and psychologist, all of which takes his time and therefore your money.

If you've had several parties catered, you probably have learned the ropes the hard way. This chapter will apprise the first-time-catered-party-thrower of what to expect and demand from the caterer. You'll also learn a trick for cutting your catering tab right down the middle.

The price can vary tremendously depending on your choice of caterer, the season (holiday parties cost more because of the high demand), and, of course, the type of food and liquor you request. Caterers don't usually like to give you any prices over the phone. However, if you sound like you know what you're talking about (and like someone the caterer would like to work with), you can get a ballpark figure. To quote my favorite caterer, "I always add a 10 percent 'Aggravation Fee' if the customer on the phone sounds like he's going to give me a hassle. I can tell right up front if he's going to be a pain in the shinbone or not." So when you place your call to the prospective caterer, be respectful of his time. Get right to the bottom line. Tell him:

1.) The date of your reception.
2.) The day of the week and the time of day.
3.) How long it is expected to last.
4.) Very important—whether it's "sit-down" or buffet. If it's sit-down, tell him what type of service. (For those of us who thrive on esoteric food facts, "American" is having all the food on the plate served to the guest. "Russian" is servers going around with individual servings. "French" is like Russian but with fancy little table-side preparations before the guest, like deboning a fish or mixing a salad.) Naturally, the more work for the servers, the higher your tab.
5.) How many guests and whether male or female.
6.) The type of food and liquor.
7.) Whether or not you want the caterer to handle decorations.

When you shoot out these facts before he has to extract them, he'll think you really know the ropes. And by now, you and I both know how much the ropes can pull down the price.

Word to the wise: call your party a RECEPTION. The caterer doesn't care whether it's a wedding, a christening or a bar mitzvah. It's all generically a "reception" to him. More insiders' jargon—your bar to him is a BAR SETUP. The place where your guests get their buffet food, coffee, dessert, anything, is a SERVING STATION . You'll really be speaking "Caterese" if your tell him how many bar setups and serving stations you envision.

Did you think it was superfluous when I suggested you tell him the sex of the guests? It wasn't. The reason your caterer needs to know is because that affects the kind of food he'll encourage you to buy. A caterer will tell you that men like heavy beefy food like big slabs of meat and cold cuts, whereas, they say, "women like to push little bits of dainty food around on a plate." (They haven't seen me eat at a party or they might have to alter their testimony.)

If the caterer's price is in your ballpark, meet with him. Discuss various types of food and beverage and then ask him to make up a price list with each food and service itemized. He might balk at this, but you are entitled to know what you are paying for each particular.

When you get the breakdown, analyze it, keeping in mind that you should be able to choose any combination of his offerings. The usual markup is as follows:

Food: 100%.
Labor: 50% to 100% depending on type of service.
Liquor: 10%.
Wine: 20%.
Disposables: varies, depending on quality. Rented china is about twice the price of the less elegant disposables. You can cut down on your tab if you have your own china and serving dishes.
Decorations: Can range from 35% to 100%.

The price he quotes you is based on his seeing your party through to its conclusion. But here's the real catering bonanza the thrifty set has been awaiting. If you know competent people who can serve at your party, you can cut your tally in two. The magic question here is, "How much will you charge for FOOD SETUP AND DELIVERY only?" If you choose this option, the caterer will come to your place and do everything except have personnel at your reception to see it through. If you live near a culinary school or have a lot of competent and reliable friends or relatives you can depend on, you can save a bundle. The caterer may not be too happy about it because he loses so much in markup, but he'll probably go with it rather than lose the job. If it's a buffet party, you hardly need any help anyway. You can further save their cleanup and pickup charges if you tell them you'll return their dishes to them clean.

Whether you're going this discount route or choosing the traditional fully catered party, it is important for you to request a refund on any liquor with unbroken seals and unchilled wine. When you chill white wine, chances are the label on the bottle is going to float way, so it's unreturnable. After your big bash, you may be drinking white wine for some time. Look at it as a good complement to the mountains of leftovers which you are also entitled to keep.

Tax and gratuities are also out of your pocket. The caterer can factor the tips into his price, but you might prefer to handle those directly with the help after the party. If you're going to do that, however, stay relatively sober. Catering help have regaled me with stories of genial drunken hosts who, after a great bacchanale, have thrown around hundred dollar bills like confetti.

If you're not quite sure how many guests are going to show up, make an estimate and confirm with the caterer that he will be prepared for the overages. Especially in the winter, it's a good idea to discuss frozen foods for the party. This way, if there is an unexpected snowstorm, you can arrange only to pay for prepared food and food that had to be thawed for the party. If your caterer can keep the frozen food in his freezer for his next reception, you should not have to pay for it. But nail this down ahead of time. If you're arranging a giant-size soiree and are worried, there are now special party cancellation insurance policies!

Speaking of insurance, if any of your guests take a shine to something belonging to your caterer, he should be covered. Ask about pilferage of any of your possessions also. You should inquire about your caterer's insurance. A good one will have liability for your guests' safety and product liability. That

How to Throw a Catered Party 169

means that if 14 of your guests go retching out the door squealing for the stomach pump, it's on him.

Finally, if you've chosen full service, tell your caterer that you do not intend to be a worried host or hostess. You want to be a guest at your own party. That way, the catering staff will know that they are responsible for *everything* you signed up for, so you can relax and enjoy your party.

If you've chosen the "food setup and delivery" route, you may be a nervous wreck afterward, but perhaps a happy one knowing how much money you've saved.

Major Savings on Major Purchases

My non-clinical research has determined that one of the greatest causes of insomnia in this country is not tension, fatigue or poor health. It's lying awake at night worrying about money—as in greenbacks, dough, gelt, cabbage. How much we've got and how much we're spending.

We awaken at night shaking from nightmares about a kangaroo court jury of expensive air-conditioners, refrigerators, stereos, and washing machines pointing accusing fingers at us and sentencing us to the poorhouse.

We can't just refuse to buy them. Our culture has convinced us that all of these appliances (and many more) are necessities of life. I'm not prepared to argue that point. But I am able to give you some sleep-filled nights and the blissful feeling of answering "Absolutely Not" to the nagging question, "Am I getting ripped off?"

If you follow this advice, it is almost guaranteed that you will be getting the *best* product for the *best* price available to you.

As with any product purchase, you first do your soul searching: "Do I really need/want this television, food processor, luggage, lawn mower, garbage disposal...whatever?" If you're like the rest of us mortals, chances are your answer will be a "Yes." Your very next step is to consult the consumer's Bible. It goes under the name of *Consumer Reports*. Issues of

Major Savings on Major Purchases

the magazine and the annual *Buying Guide* summarizing the year's findings can be found in practically every library in the country. Or you can write to them at: Consumers Union, Dept. DCB-LF, 256 Washington Street, Mt. Vernon, N.Y. 10553.

Consulting *Consumer Reports* can save you countless hours of traipsing from store to store doing your own informal market research. By reading their descriptions and little charts, you will be an instant expert on any product's quality, performance, price, advantages and disadvantages. Next time you're shopping for luggage, instead of tugging on a suitcase's handle to see how secure it feels to you, depend on the guys who have tugged on the luggage handles of all major brands with big machines at least 2,500 times each.

From talking with a main man at Consumers Union (the company which publishes *Consumer Reports*), I got the idea that working there must be like having a desk in the middle of a six-ring circus. As a Consumers Union secretary walks in to work, she goes to an undistinguished brick building squeezed between a public utility plant and a smelting plant in Mt. Vernon, New York. But that's where the "undistinguished" ends. At this writing, outside the building there are a dozen extension ladders with guys scurrying up and down them to test their strength. As our secretary starts her journey to her desk, she walks down the halls piled high with shipments of products from all across the country. The first thing she hears is a series of thunderous thudding noises coming from a room which has a giant mallet pounding on mattresses to test their durability. She passes a room which has an enormous clothes-dryer-type machine filled with suitcases churning and bouncing around in it to test their strength. As she continues down the hall, the thudding segues into loud rock music from compact disc players being tested. Finally, you might think you've come upon the company's gym. No, it's a room with a bunch of engineers working out to test exercise equipment. This whole vaudeville act is very serious and scientific stuff designed to help you judge which luggage, mattress, disc player and exercise equipment you should buy.

Everyone at Consumers Union (CU) gets into the act—secretaries, mail room clerks and top executives. The CU staff has been known to overdose on angel food cake during oven testings, get the jitters during coffee testings and go grungy for days wearing the same clothes during detergent testings. They were saved from being told to catch a cold for a tissue testing by the CU engineers' unique invention of the highly acclaimed Sneeze Machine, which shoots nose-size blasts of heaven knows what concoction into tissues.

All of this is to say, "With almost anything you're buying, leave the initial comparison to them." Once shown the models of choice by CU, the purchasing path you then pursue is dependent on the type of merchandise you are buying. Let's start with:

STEREOS

After you have an indication of the type of equipment you want, call a few local stereo stores and, if they carry the receiver and speakers (and turntable, cassette deck, compact disc player or whatever else you want), ask if they have a space where you can listen to them. Many stores will have a room set aside for just this; others have a wall of speakers that can be plugged into the various receivers. Then clean out your ears, and go for a listen. This is an important step if you're interested in quality, because what constitutes "good" sound can be very subjective. All speakers have different sound characteristics.

Do not panic when you look at the price tag of the equipment you want. You are probably going to pay only a little over half—at the most two-thirds—of their cost. How?

Major Savings on Major Purchases

(Our source here is a 16-year-old rock music buff named "Gus"—freckles, bright red long curly ringlets, very big ears and a good eye for stereo bargains.) Here's how.

Let me preface this advice by giving my sincere apologies to stereo store owners across the country who understandably are going to want to ban this book. What you do is write down the brand and model number of the equipment you want, thank your local stereo store clerk for his hospitality and go buy a copy of one of the "music rags." There are several—*High Fidelity* and *Stereo Review* are good sources. Finger through them and find the ads for the big wholesale outlets. There are always several with 800 numbers. Call them and get quotes on the exact model numbers you want. Because they do a huge volume, have little overhead and don't have to spend the time with you that our patient sales clerk did in choosing your equipment, they can afford to give tremendous discounts.

You will be amazed—nay, *shocked*—at the savings you can get. I checked it out. It's all true. I found prices 30 percent to 50 percent below list! You place your order and within a week or two you will receive your favorite gramophone in its factory-sealed box, manufacturer's warranty and all.

APPLIANCES

The strategy here is a little different. After you have a pretty clear idea of the refrigerator, clothes dryer, television set, air-conditioner or whatever you want, your first step is to invest zero cents in a toll-free call to AT&T's 800-Information. See if the manufacturer has an 800 number. Most of the biggies like Westinghouse and General Electric generally do.

Ask the 800 number folks what authorized dealers they have in the area. And then, ask anything else you want to know about the appliance. Depending on the size of the appliance, don't forget to ask about the energy efficiency. A blooper on a big appliance—especially one that generates heat or cold—could cost you hundreds of dollars a year in energy costs. Over the lifetime of a refrigerator, it costs more to run than to buy!

Nowadays, most major appliances have "energy labels" posted on them which tell you how much it costs to run that appliance for one year. You have to have a few cognitive and interpretive skills to understand them, but exercise a little concentration and all will become clear. It is important in figuring your "better deal" to factor in the cost of running the darn thing.

Visit a dealer and fondle the appliance a little, see if it is right for you or your home, and get whatever information you want from the salesman. By the way, be real nice to the poor chap because the joy of your personality is probably all he's going to get from you this time. To assuage your conscience, if he's been especially helpful, you can write a complimentary letter to his boss. Do *something* nice, because what you are about to do now saves you a lot of money but is not the nicest thing to do to your conscientious clerk.

When your decision is firm, call the various discount and outlet houses in your area. They are easy to ferret out by simply asking around, checking the Yellow Pages and keeping an eye out for the ads in local newspapers.

Model number in hand, check a few prices on the phone. If a nasal voice says, "Company policy is we don't give prices," tell Nasal Voice, "Look, is it company policy not to sell? I'm definitely going to buy a Big Widget, model number 007, and if you can give me the best price, I'll drive out today and pick it up." If she stonewalls you, ask for the manager. Your argument will usually work like a can opener on the owner or manager of the discount store.

Giant discount/outlet stores claim—and give—discounts in the 10 percent to 35 percent range. How can they do it? It's certainly not "hot" merchandise. But sometimes it can be a

Major Savings on Major Purchases

little "warm" through a cozy arrangement with various sources.

There are a myriad of perfectly legal reasons that certain stores can give hefty discounts. A lot of outlet stores get appliances that were used in cooking shows or as demonstrator models in other stores. Or perhaps the discount store made a killing on a discontinued model. There can be big savings on what is called "scratch and dent" merchandise. These are wares that might have a tiny scratch on them, thereby prohibiting them from wearing a higher price tag.

The only minor wrinkle in buying from certain super-discounted stores is that some are not "Authorized Factory Dealers" and therefore you *might* have a problem with the warranty. It's a slim chance, however, and one well worth taking. Most things don't break down, especially ones with good performance records. (You checked that out in *Consumer Reports*, remember?) And to get most factory guarantees, all you need to prove is the date of purchase.

By the way, have you, like me, wasted hours of your life filling out those little warranty cards? Forget it. They are meaningless except for the manufacturer's market research! Just hang on to your little dated sales slip.

To guard against getting a "lemon," put the following codicil on your sales slip: "May be exchanged within two days if not operating satisfactorily." If it's a big item which has to be delivered, substitute "Will be exchanged at store's expense if not..." Have your salesman initial it.

You are now ready for the final step. That is giving yourself a big pat on the back that you have the best appliance, at the best price, with the best performance record, and with the best savings in energy. Congratulations.

CAMERAS AND CAMERA EQUIPMENT

I never cease to be amazed at certain people's sophistication concerning apertures and *f*-stops—and their lack of sophistication on how to get a much better deal on their new cameras.

Unless you're buying a real cheapie plastic camera (the descendant of the old "Brownie"), chances are you at least know enough to know what you want. If not, you can check Consumers Union's ratings on cameras and visit various camera stores with photography experts on staff. Do all the research and question-asking you like, but when it comes time to buy, the way is uncontested.

Turn to one of the Pro's Paradises. There are two—*Modern Photography* and *Popular Photography* magazines. Flip through the pages and therein find mail-order houses which do such a tremendous volume that they can offer spectacular savings on top name equipment. The discounts are hard to believe. The only requirement of you is that you must know exactly what you want. They have no time for the question-asking browser. *The Sunday New York Times* also advertises some high-quality, low-low-priced outlets. Why would anybody buy camera equipment any other way?

CLOTHING

Personally, I'm addicted to all of the beautiful gowns, cashmere sweaters, and sequined bags that one can dig up for a song in archaeological expeditions through thrift shops. However, if you prefer your antiques on the mantelpiece rather than on your back, there are great thrifty alternatives. But before I get off my favorite store-category, let me sing one more chorus of praise for second-hand clothing stores (for all but business clothing).

As anybody who has ever looked at the price tags can attest, tremendous bargains are to be found in thrift stores. There are two kinds of stores: charity and consignment. The stock in charity shops is from donations and the proceeds go to various charities. People who "donate" to consignment stores are hoping that the shop will sell their merchandise and then the profits will be shared. You'll find lower prices and quality in

Major Savings on Major Purchases

charity stores (but feel more philanthropic shopping there). The converse is true for consignment stores.

Thrift stores make special sense for families with growing children, since a year after purchase, the clothes no longer fit. Next to phenomenal prices, the biggest advantage to thrift stores is that you actually see what the blouse or dress looks like after several washings or cleanings—always a mystery with new clothing.

If you're squeamish or your lifestyle does not fit into taking advantage of this type of bargain, let me touch on some other better deals you can get and then I'll refer you to another book if you want to pursue it further.

People are getting very, very price conscious. And (hurrah for supply and demand) business is responding. There are a multitude of factory outlet shops and malls, discount centers, mail-order houses and manufacturers' outlets cropping up all over. Clothing is the biggie item, but there are also outlets which offer records, shoes, towels, china, handbags, curtains, blankets, pots and pans and, yes, kitchen sinks. There are discounts on name merchandise—and even designer clothes—from 30 percent to 75 percent off list, all to be had by the man or woman who knows where to find them. The stores get their merchandise from:

Closeout Sales
  Designer Original Samples (designer's inspirations that never made it)
    Irregulars or Seconds
    Job Lots purchased due to bankruptcy or damage
      Knockoffs (quite simply, rip-off copies of designer clothes)
        Carryovers (last year's goods)

The term that is being coined for all of this is OFF PRICING. If saving money turns you on, let me refer you to two directories of discount stores which you can find in the library or your bookstore. One is *Bird's Guide to Bargain Shopping*, published by Andrews, McMeel, Parker, and the other is the *Underground Shopper's Guide to Off-Price Shopping*, published by Warner Books. In each, you will find hundreds of outlets listed with name, address, phone number and the type of merchandise offered.

BUYING CLUBS

Another frugal-family dream is the "Buying Club." Check your local Chamber of Commerce to see which buying clubs might be in your area. They are similar to food buying clubs, but cover a wider range of products.

I can't go into specifics here because each one differs in range of products, discounts and membership requirements, but they are definitely worth looking into. The largest and oldest—and of national scope—is the United Buying Service at 415 Lexington Avenue in New York City.

OTHER BIG PURCHASES

Other major purchases like rotary lawn mowers, gas barbecue grills, small farm equipment, and the like can be found at big farm or hardware stores. So yet another strategy for getting a better deal is called into play. It's an age-old art almost forgotten in today's retail society, but it works in owner-run stores which sell big ticket items. In certain cultures it's called "haggling." I prefer "negotiating."

Many people know that it is de rigueur to haggle with new car salesmen. So why should it be any different dealing with a Big Widget salesman? The only truly effective way to arrive at the lowest price for a car is to know the dealer's cost or "invoice price." The dealer's cost for the Big Widget is also invaluable knowledge but a little harder to find because, unlike cars, no one publishes the figures on Widgetry.

To be effective in any negotiation, you must be armed with the accurate name, specs and model number of the wanted

Widget. If you take the salesman's time inquiring about every little whimma-ditty about the Widget, he figures two things—both right. One, you should pay for the time he's spent with you. And two, you don't know a heck of a lot about the product. Therefore, he calculates, you don't know that he has any margin to play with on the price. Shop around and ask your questions at other stores—not the one you intend to get the good price from.

Then go to the shop you want to buy from and say, "I'll buy Big Widget, model number PQ 20112-A, from you if you can knock 15 percent off." It will probably work, but if he says no, you've fired your last shot except for telling the owner or manager the same thing. It's better to have another round.

Here's a little more powder and shot. First call the manufacturer—preferably on his 800 number—and ask him what "distributors" (not dealers) service your area. By the way, while you have the manufacturer on the line, ask any other questions you have about the product.

With the model number and distributor scribbled on a piece of paper, you have another chance. Let's say you're dealing with an $800 Widget. When the salesman says he can't move on price, you come back with, "Look, I know Charlie up at SupplyAll couldn't be charging you that much. I'll pay you his cost, your delivery cost, and another $60. That's not bad. You'll make sixty dollars for one phone call." He'll be aghast that you know his distributor's name. He'll also assume you're so well connected that "Charlie" would probably sell it to you direct, so why not make his little profit?

It's also helpful to know what your salesman's situation is: Is he on commission, does he own the store, or is he on straight salary? Some salesmen get commissions on the top of the line items only (or higher commissions on them), so they have an interest in upgrading your purchase. You can ask him if he gets commission on the Bigger Widget, and, if the product's any good for you, you can always offer to buy that one if he'll give you a greater discount.

If you really want to get the haggling award of the year, you can do the following—but only if you enjoy the sport of it. Before you go to the store and when you have the distributor on the line, say, "This is Tom Smythe. I have a customer who has requested a Widget, model number PQ 20112-A. Could you give me dealer and list price?"

You're not lying; you *are* a customer. You'd really be fudging it if you said, "This is Tom from Smythe's Appliances," so I'm not advising that. However, be aware that distributors prefer to give prices only to dealers, so the more professional you sound, the more apt you are to get the phone quote. I've never had a problem getting one.

Now you're invincible. You know his price and can make just the right offer. It can be well below list as long as it's enough above cost to make it worth his while.

By the way, there are more direct ways to get your dealer's cost. If you feel comfortable with it, you can ask him what it is! Otherwise, ask for his catalogue—not the one for customers. Find the chart of dealer and list costs for each item in the back. If he has his catalogue on "microfiche" (that's a version of microfilm), his price will be on the same page as the specs. It may be couched in code, but it's a pretty easy one to crack after you've looked at a page or two. Look for a number around 20-40 percent below list price and that's probably it. Or, if it's a number between 20 and 40, there's a good chance that the catalogue is telling how many percentage points dealer's cost is below list.

If your salesman seems at all hesitant to move on price, mention that he might want to consult with the manger or owner. And they'll usually take your "something" above cost rather than nothing.

I want to give you a parting reminder. The days of the Arab market are not a thing of the past. They are very much alive and well in contemporary American owner-run stores which sell big ticket items—for those who know how to deal.

Appendix

DON'T STORE LONGER THAN...

Food	Don't Store Longer than
FRUITS	10–12 months
VEGETABLES	10–12 months
MEATS	
Bacon (sliced)	1 month
Bacon (unsliced)	2–4 months
Beef	10–12 months
Chicken, Ducks, Capons, Geese	12 months
Fish (lean)—bass, perch, pike, sunfish, trout	6–8 months
Fish (fatty)—catfish, herring, mackerel, salmon, shrimp, whitefish	2–4 months
Ground beef	4–6 months
Ham	3–4 months
Pork	4–6 months
Pheasant, Quail, Grouse, etc.	6 months
Sausage (seasoned)	2 months
Sausage (unsalted)	4–6 months
Variety meats (heart, kidney, liver, tongue)	1 month
DAIRY PRODUCTS	
Butter	4–6 months
Cheese (hard only—soft can't be frozen)	4–5 months

Food	Don't Store Longer than
Cream	3–4 months
Eggs (break and mix them)	10–12 months
BAKED PRODUCTS	
Bread and rolls	2–3 months
Cakes (frosted)	2 months
Cakes (unfrosted)	3–4 months
Pies (baked)	1 month
Pies (unbaked)	1–2 months
MISCELLANEOUS	
Ice Cream (original carton)	1 month
Left-Overs (cooked)	1 month
Soups, Stews, Casseroles	2–3 months

WHEN IT'S GOOD AND CHEAP...

JANUARY
   Avocados, Bananas, Broccoli, Brussels Sprouts, Cabbage, Carrots, Celery, Grapefruit, Lettuce, Mushrooms, Onions, Oranges, Potatoes, Spinach, Turnips.

FEBRUARY
   Avocados, Bananas, Broccoli, Brussels Sprouts, Cabbage, Carrots, Celery, Grapefruit, Lettuce, Mushrooms, Oranges, Peas, Potatoes, Spinach, Turnips.

MARCH
   Artichokes, Asparagus, Avocados, Bananas, Broccoli, Cabbage, Carrots, Celery, Grapefruit, Lettuce, Mushrooms, Onions, Oranges, Peas, Pineapples, Potatoes, Radishes, Spinach, Turnips.

APRIL
   Artichokes, Asparagus, Avocados, Bananas, Broccoli, Cabbage, Carrots, Celery, Grapefruit, Lettuce, Mushrooms, Onions, Oranges, Peas, Pineapples, Potatoes, Radishes, Spinach, Strawberries, Watercress.

Appendix

MAY
Artichokes, Asparagus, Avocados, Bananas, Beans (green), Cabbage, Carrots, Celery, Corn, Cucumbers, Lemons, Lettuce, Mushrooms, Onions, Oranges, Papayas, Peas, Pineapples, Potatoes, Radishes, Strawberries, Tomatoes, Watercress, Watermelons.

JUNE
Apricots, Asparagus, Bananas, Beans (green), Beets, Blackberries, Blueberries, Cabbage, Cantaloupes, Carrots, Celery, Cherries, Corn, Cucumbers, Honeydew Melons, Lemons, Lettuce, Limes, Mushrooms, Nectarines, Onions, Papayas, Peas, Peaches, Peppers (green), Pineapples, Plums, Potatoes, Radishes, Raspberries, Squash, Strawberries, Tomatoes, Watercress, Watermelons.

JULY
Apricots, Bananas, Beans (green), Beets, Blackberries, Blueberries, Cabbage, Cantaloupes, Celery, Cherries, Corn, Cucumbers, Grapes, Honeydew Melons, Lemons, Lettuce, Limes, Nectarines, Onions, Papayas, Peas, Peaches, Peppers (green), Pineapples, Plums, Potatoes, Radishes, Raspberries, Squash, Tomatoes, Watercress, Watermelons.

AUGUST
Beans (green), Beets, Blueberries, Cantaloupes, Corn, Cucumbers, Eggplant, Grapes, Honeydew Melons, Lemons, Lettuce, Limes, Nectarines, Onions, Peaches, Pears, Peppers (green), Pineapples, Plums, Potatoes, Squash, Tomatoes, Watermelons.

SEPTEMBER
Apples, Beets, Cabbage, Cantaloupes, Carrots, Cauliflower, Coconuts, Corn, Eggplant, Grapes, Honeydew Melons, Lettuce, Nectarines, Onions, Peaches, Pears, Peppers (green), Plums, Potatoes, Squash, Sweet Potatoes.

OCTOBER
Apples, Avocados, Bananas, Beets, Brussels Sprouts, Cabbage, Carrots, Cauliflower, Celery, Coconuts, Cranberries, Eggplant,

Grapes, Honeydew Melons, Lettuce, Mushrooms, Onions, Papayas, Pears, Potatoes, Squash, Sweet Potatoes, Turnips.

NOVEMBER
Apples, Avocados, Bananas, Broccoli, Brussels Spouts, Cabbage, Carrots, Cauliflower, Celery, Coconuts, Cranberries, Grapefruit, Grapes, Mushrooms, Onions, Papayas, Parsley, Pears, Potatoes, Squash, Sweet Potatoes, Turnips.

DECEMBER
Apples, Avocados, Bananas, Broccoli, Brussels Sprouts, Cabbage, Carrots, Celery, Coconuts, Cranberries, Grapefruit, Lettuce, Mushrooms, Onions, Oranges, Parsley, Potatoes, Sweet Potatoes, Turnips.

GLOSSARY OF INDUSTRY TERMS

The following, which we'll humbly call a "glossary," is actually a mini-language which will open the doors for bigger savings and better service for you. After you've read the book, familiarize yourself with some of the following words and word usages. Then use them when dealing with people in the appropriate industries.

Drop a few of these words, and the vendor will say to himself, "Hmmmm, if this customer knows that word, he's probably familiar with my industry inside out." This indicates to him that you probably also know his best price and the best service that's available.

A-V—When a lawyer refers to another lawyer or law firm as A-V, he means "top drawer." Every lawyer and law firm of note is rated in a book (which all law libraries have) called *Martindale Hubbell*. "A" means excellent legal ability and "V" stands for very high ethical standards.

ACCESSORIAL CHARGE—To folks in the moving business, this means extra charges to you for any difficulty in getting your furniture and goods from their truck to your house.

Appendix

AFFIDAVITS—Generally an affidavit is a sworn statement. In the radio biz, it's the listing of commercials that ran in any given hour.

APEX—This is a special inexpensive airline fare that has certain travel restrictions.

ASSIGNED RISK—If an auto-insurance salesman considers you an accident looking to happen, he'll put you in an "assigned risk" category and your premium will be very expensive.

BALLOON PACKING—When the moving van boys pack your boxes half full of your goods and then pack the rest with stuffing so they can call it a full box, they are guilty of "balloon packing."

BILL OF LADING— "Mover-ese" for "receipt." It also includes details of your contract.

BILLABLE HOURS—This is what lawyers call the hours they charge their clients for.

BILLED NUMBER SCREENING—A service you can request from the phone company so that any collect and third party calls can be intercepted.

BINDING ESTIMATE—A price estimate that the vendor cannot exceed. A "not-to-exceed" binding estimate is offered by some moving companies which charge by weight.

BLANKET—To your furrier, a "blanket" is a big piece of fur sewn together from smaller skins to form the material that the coat is made from.

BUFFALO—An old work-horse of a General Motors bus which is very popular in the bus-chartering business. Also known as "deck and a half."

BULK SPOT SCHEDULE—The radio advertising boys refer to a large number of commercials purchased as a "bulk spot schedule."

CALL ME CARD—Also called a "Call Home" card. A card issued by the phone company that you give to the folks who call you collect. You save because it's less expensive than a regular collect call.

CAMERA READY—What artists and printers call the artwork and copy that is ready to be reproduced by the printer's camera.

CAPE—A diamond isn't "yellowish" in the diamond world. It's "cape."

CAPTIVE AGENT—An auto insurance agent who either works for a big insurance company and sells only their policies, or an independent agent who is contracted to sell insurance from one insurer only.

CHARTER—If you want a good price when renting a bus, don't say "renting." Tell them you want to "charter" it.

CLOSER—You'll find them in many industries. They are professional salesmen who excel at closing the sale.

COLLISION—Auto insurance coverage for your car in accidents where you are at fault.

COLOR BREAK—Painters refer to one color flush up against another as a "color break."

COLOR CORRECTED—A term meaning that colors have been made to conform to the correct color in a photograph—that is, grass is made green.

COMPREHENSIVE—Auto insurance coverage including fire, theft, vandalism, glass breakage, etc.

CSR—Customer Service Representative. Many industries have Customer Service Reps. We talk about how they can help you in the travel chapter.

CUSTOM LAB—A photography lab which takes special care in processing photographs instead of just developing them without looking at them.

CUTTING IN—This is what painters call the work involved in putting one color next to another. It forms what they call a "color break."

DEADHEADING—Practically every industry involved with travel uses this term. It means an airplane, bus or ship is going from one place to another without passengers.

Appendix

DEALER PREPARATION—Also called "Dealer Prep." It's the costs the auto salesmen charge for "preparing" the car for you—consisting of putting hub caps on, washing it, you name it. Basically it can be a hidden profit.

DEALER PRICE—The price a dealer pays for goods. Knowing this price is an all-important tool in your negotiations.

DECLARATION SHEET—This is the top sheet of your homeowner's insurance policy that gives you, in a nutshell, what coverage you have.

DELIVERY SPREAD—The way a moving company refers to the time between picking your stuff up and delivering it to you.

DESTINATION—Using this term when talking with pros in the bus chartering or moving business will brand you as someone who knows the ropes. It means, of course, the place where passengers or goods are dropped off.

DESTINATION CHARGE—This is the cost that the auto dealer pays for the car to be delivered from wherever it was manufactured to his dealership.

DISPUTE—A "dispute" to the Credit Rating Bureaus means you don't agree with their judgment of your credit-worthiness. You're allowed to contest it.

DRAFT AUTHORITY—This is an interesting advantage that certain auto and homeowner's insurance salesmen have from the insuring company. It means they can write you a check right off the insuring company's checkbook (up to a certain limit) for your claim.

DRESSED—It makes a great deal of difference to a furrier where a fur was "dressed" —in other words, where the skins were cleaned and prepared.

EQUIPMENT INVENTORY FORM—A form which the phone company must give you upon request detailing exactly what you are paying for on the monthly bills.

EXCLUSIVE LISTING—A kind of listing that real estate brokers have, giving that broker exclusive rights to sell that particular piece of property.

FACT SHEET—This term is used in many industries. In radio advertising, it's the page of information that the radio DJ or host uses to get information about a product.

FARE PROTECTION—An airline good-deal which permits you to purchase your ticket far in advance of your trip, thereby protecting you from fare increases.

FEATHERS—"Feathers" to a jeweler are little flaws in a gem.

FLOATER—This is any addition to the basic homeowner's insurance policy. When you're dealing with life or health insurance, it's called a "Rider." The auto insurance boys call the same thing an "Endorsement."

FOOD SET UP AND DELIVERY—This is the phrase to use with your caterer when you simply want him to prepare the food and deliver it to your house.

GIT FARES—Airlines and travel agents talk about Group Inclusive Tour fares—or "GIT Fares." They are super cheap fares that you can get for both airfare and land arrangements if you are part of a group.

GLETZ—A jeweler refers to a little imperfection in a stone as a "Gletz." Also called an "Inclusion."

GRID CARD—Also referred to as a "Rate Card." This is the price list for radio advertising—always priced at top dollar.

HOLIDAY—To your house or apartment painter, a "holiday" is not a vacation. It's an undone spot or a spot not covered well with paint.

HOMEOWNERS 1, 2 or 3—This is the way the homeowner's insurance boys (and the knowledgeable buyers) refer to the policies. HO 1 is minimum coverage, HO 2 is recommended for most of us ordinary folk, HO 3 covers just about any catastrophe a sci-fi writer could conjure up.

INCLUSION—See "Gletz."

IN-SERVICE TIME—This is the way that the travel industry refers to the time that the plane, train, bus or limo takes from "origin" to "destination."

INVOICE PRICE—In the auto industry, the "invoice price" is the tab that the dealer pays to the manufacturer for the car.

INWARD OPERATOR—The operator you should ask for when you're having trouble calling overseas. It's an operator in the country being called.

IT PACKAGE—Travel agents talk about Inclusive Tour fares which cover both airfare and land arrangements.

JOBBER PRICE—The price that a volume dealer pays for the goods. A very large garage would get "jobber" prices on auto parts. Your local gas pumper with one mechanic would get "dealer" prices. The customer usually gets "list," unless he knows how to ask for something better.

KEYSTONE—Also called "K." This is the word that people in the jewelry business use when they mean "double the price." For instance, if a jeweler tells another jeweler in front of you that the price is $200K, that means it will cost him $100, leaving his option open to charge you $200. Triple Keystone means three times the price. Many jewelry catalogues are written in 3K.

LABOR MANUAL—Almost every auto repair shop has a labor manual—different publishers but all essentially the same. The labor manual tells the mechanic (and you should look at it) how long any car repair should take for purposes of labor charges.

LETTERPRESS—A printing process—the old-fashioned kind where a press actually presses the ink onto the paper.

LINE MAN—The bus industry refers to a driver who is not necessarily experienced in dealing with people as a "line man."

LIST PRICE—The full consumer's price.

LISTING AGENCY—Real estate brokers can get this status from a house seller. It means that they are the "primary" broker but the house is also on "multiple listings."

LONG HAUL CHARGE—The way the moving boys refer to your basic tab (usually done by weight) for moving your goods from "origin" to "destination."

LOUPE—This is the little magnifying glass that a jeweler puts in his eye to look more closely at a gem.

MAKE GOOD—A radio or television commercial that is played ("runs") because the first one was missed.

MECHANICAL—To a printer, a "mechanical" is the "camera ready" finished product that he shoots from.

MULTIPLE LISTING—If your real estate broker has a house on "multiple listing," it means that some other broker has it on "primary" but he can sell it to you anyway.

NEST—Jewelers do not think of birds when they hear "nest." To them a nest is a grouping of little imperfections in a stone.

NON-STANDARD—A polite word in the auto insurance industry for "sub-standard." It's an insurance category for those deemed more likely to have an accident than the "preferred." More expensive, of course.

OFFSET—A printing process in which the artwork is photo-reproduced, but better than Xerox.

ORIGIN—In industries such as moving and bus chartering, the "origin" is the place the truck or bus starts.

PARTY—To a restaurateur, your group is a "party." Party of two, party of four, etc.

PBO—Packed By Owner. The moving van boys refer to any boxes packed by you (the owner) as "PBO."

PERFORMANCE RECORD—This is the Interstate Commerce Commisison's "report card" on van lines. It is available to you for the asking. It tells how many shipments that moving company made in the last year and how many complaints were received about them.

PIECE COAT—The fur industry calls a coat made from smaller pieces of fur sewn together a "piece coat."

POLITICAL RATE—The cheapest rate that a radio station is

Appendix

permitted to sell a commercial for. The politicians get this rate when they advertise around election time.

PRE-NEED—A term devised by the funeral industry, which means making funeral arrangements before death.

PREFERRED—The best auto-insurance category. You should try to find an agent who will put you in this least expensive category. It's cheapest because it means, in your agent's estimation, that you are least likely to have an accident.

PREPPING—A painter's preparation of the surfaces to be painted.

PROMOTIONAL FARE—The airlines offer a certain number of seats on a plane at a discount so that the low fare can be advertised.

RATE CARD—See "Grid Card."

RATING TERRITORY—Auto insurance companies rate areas of the country by traffic congestion, super highways, etc. The price you pay for auto insurance is in part dependent on the past and projected susceptibility to accidents of drivers in the area in which you reside.

RECEPTION—No matter what kind of bash you are throwing, your caterer refers to it as a "reception."

RIDER—See "Floater."

RUN OF STATION—A commercial that is played at whatever time the station chooses.

SCRAPING AND SPACKLING—Almost sounds like one word when painters say "scraping'n'spackling." It's what they do to prepare the walls for paint.

SERVING STATION—Your caterer refers to any place your guests pick up food or drink as a "serving station."

SHORT RATE—A method of pro-rating insurance charges on cancelled policies that charges more toward the beginning of the policy so the customer gets short-changed if he cancels.

SPOT PRIME—When your painter has to fix up certain spots before painting, he's "spot priming."

STANDARD—The auto insurance category that your agent will put you in if you don't qualify for "preferred." It means he thinks you're more likely to have an accident than his preferred customers, and your premiums will be higher.

TARE WEIGHT—The weight of the empty moving van before your goods are loaded.

TARIFF—The price that moving companies and bus chartering companies must have on file with the ICC.

TOUR MAN—When you get a "tour man" on your chartered bus, you're getting a driver experienced in working with people. Ask for one.

TRANSFER LETTERING—A do-it-yourselfer's dream. "Transfer lettering" is an acetate filled with letters of the alphabet which you can transfer to your paper to look like professionally set headlines.

TYPEFACE—The different styles of lettering are called "typefaces."

UNRESTRICTED COACH—The most expensive coach airline seat there is. There are no restrictions on the travel dates.

FUNERAL HOME, INC.

GENERAL PRICE LIST

These Prices are Effective as of _____

The merchandise and services shown on this list are those we can provide to our clients. You may choose only those items you desire. However, any funeral selections you make will include a charge for our services. If legal or other requirements mean that you must purchase any items not specifically requested, we will explain the reasons for this in writing. This will be shown on the Statement of Funeral Goods & Services Selected.

This list does not include prices for any items that you ask us to purchase, such as cemetery or crematory services, flowers and newspaper notices. The prices for such items will be shown on your Statement of Funeral Goods & Services Selected. We will   charge you for arranging for or purchasing these items.

•••

FORWARDING OF REMAINS TO ANOTHER FUNERAL HOME .... $ 775.00
    This charge includes removal of remains, services of staff, Base necessary authorizations, embalming, use of facilities & local Local transportation (but not shipping charges).

RECEIVING OF REMAINS FROM ANOTHER FUNERAL HOME .... $ 590.00
    This charge includes services of staff, care of remains, use of facilities (excl. visitation & funeral ceremony), transportation to funeral home & casket coach to cemetery or crematory.

DIRECT CREMATIONS: Range of Prices ..... $ 395.00 + Cash Advances
    Our charge for a direct cremation (excl. ceremony) includes removal of remains & transportation to crematory, necessary services of staff, authorizations & basic use of facilities. If you want to arrange a direct cremation, you can use an unfinished wood box or an alternative container. Alternative containers can be made of materials like heavy cardboard or composition materials (with or without outside covering), or pouches of canvas.

Direct Cremation With Unfinished Wood Box .... $ n/a
Direct Cremation With Alternative Container .... $ 445.00
Direct Cremation (Container provided by Client) .... $ *

IMMEDIATE BURIALS: Range of Prices ..... $ 525.00 + Cemetery
    Our charge for an immediate burial (excl. ceremony) includes Require. removal & care of remains, necessary staff services, authorizations, basic use of facilities & casket coach to cemetery.

Immediate Burial With Minimum Casket .... $ 936.00
Immediate Burial With Unfinished Wood Box. Particle Br... $ 525.00
Immediate Burial (Container provided by Client) .... $ *

GENERAL PRICE LIST (Continued)

FUNERAL ARRANGEMENTS:

Embalming .... $ _185.00_

> Except in certain special cases, embalming is not required by law. Embalming may be necessary, however, if you select certain funeral arrangements, such as a funeral with viewing. If you do not want embalming, you usually have the right to choose an arrangement which does not require you to pay for it, such as direct cremation or immediate burial.

Other Preparation of Body .... $ _75.00_

Use of Facilities and Equipment:
For Funeral Ceremony .... $ _125.00_
For Visitation or Viewing _each additional 75.00_ .. $ _150.00_
Preparation Room .... $ _85.00_
General Use of Facilities .... $ _75.00_
    (parking facilities, offices, lounges, storage rooms, etc.)

Transfer of Remains to Funeral Home
(within _16_ mile radius) .... $ _105.00_

Automotive Equipment:
Casket Coach (Hearse) .... $ _105.00_
Funeral Sedan .... $ _50.00_
Flower Car .... $ _45.00_
_____ $ _____
_____ $ _____
Limousine Quoted At Time of Service .... $ _____

Miscellaneous Merchandise:
Acknowledgment Cards .... _25 @ 3.75_ .... $ _____
Visitors Register .... _Hard Cover 10.00_ .... $ _____
                     Soft Cover 5.00 .... $ _____
_____ $ _____
_____ $ _____
_____ $ _____

Caskets (Range of Prices) .... $ _411.00 & Up_
    (A complete price list will be provided at the funeral home)

Outer Burial Containers (Range of Prices) ... $ _370.00-1500.00_
    (A complete price list will be provided at the funeral home)

Other:
_____ _Home Service Add 300.00_ .... $ _____
_____ _Additional Services Charged_ ...... $ _____
_____ _On Request Or If Required_ .... $ _____
_____ _By Health or Law_ .... $ _____

Services of Funeral Director and Staff .... $ _450.00_

> Our charge includes funeral counseling, arranging and directing visitation and ceremony, recording vital statistics, securing permits, filing and obtaining death certificates and other forms and claims, preparation of necessary notices, handling of flowers, presence at cemetery for interment and service to family following burial. This fee will be added to the total cost of the funeral goods and services you select. Such a fee is already included in our charges for direct cremations, immediate burials and forwarding or receiving remains.

Basic 195.00
Limited 335.00
Forward or Recv